The LIGHT of LIFE

What Are You Living for Today?

Reginald Nedzamba

KINGDOM BOOKS
Your kingdom come, your will be done

Copyright © Reginald Nedzamba, 2016

Published by Kingdom Books, an imprint of
CreativeJuicesBooks, Singapore (www.creativejuicesbooks.com)

All rights reserved. No part of this book may be reproduced, stored in a retrieval system, or transmitted in any form or by any means — electronic, mechanical, digital, photocopy, recording, or any other — except for brief quotations in printed reviews, without prior permission in writing from the publisher.

All Scripture quotations are taken from the *Holy Bible: New International Version* ®. Copyright © 1973, 1978, 1984 International Bible Society. Used by permission of Zondervan Bible Publishers. All rights reserved.

National Library Board, Singapore Cataloguing-in-Publication Data

Name(s): Nedzamba, Reginald.

Title: The light of life : what are you living for today? / Reginald Nedzamba.

Description: [Singapore] : Kingdom Books, an imprint of Creative Juices Books, [2016]

Identifier(s): OCN 950877175 | ISBN 978-981-09-9129-6 (paperback)

Subject(s): LCSH: Kingdom of God. | Christian life. | Salvation--Christianity.

Classification: DDC 231.72--dc23

Contents

	Introduction: The Truth about Life	1
1.	Your Life Belongs to God Your Maker	15
2.	It's not about the Gift but the Purpose of that Gift	24
3.	Not Your Will but His Will	32
4.	The Restoration of God's Original Plan	49
5.	You Cannot Serve Both the Spirit and the Flesh	67
6.	You Are Forgiven!	80
7.	Saved in the Name of Jesus Christ	85
8.	Every Promise Is Governed by Certain Principles	92
9.	The Secret of Our Battle	107
10.	The Keys to Your Destiny	117
11.	Destiny Is Not Instant but God's Planned Process	133
12.	God's Grace	146
	The Prayer of Repentance	151

INTRODUCTION

The Truth about Life

Now the serpent was more crafty than any of the wild animals the LORD God had made. He said to the woman, "Did God really say, 'You must not eat from any tree in the garden'?"

The woman said to the serpent, "We may eat fruit from the trees in the garden, but God did say, 'You must not eat fruit from the tree that is in the middle of the garden, and you must not touch it, or you will die.'"

"You will not surely die," the serpent said to the woman. "For God knows that when you eat of it your eyes will be opened, and you will be like God, knowing good and evil."

When the woman saw that the fruit of the tree was good for food and pleasing to the eye, and also desirable for gaining wisdom, she took some and ate it. She also gave some to her husband, who was with her, and he ate it. Then the eyes of both of them were opened, and they realized they were naked; so they sewed fig leaves together and made coverings for themselves.

Genesis 3:1-7

When you buy a bottle of Coca-Cola®, you gain the right of ownership over it, and you have the right to store your own product in it. In the same way, the devil purchased the right of ownership over man when Adam and Eve sold themselves to him; and that gave him the right to store his own product in man.

THE LIGHT OF LIFE

In the Garden of Eden, God lost His rights of ownership over His own vessel (man) when Adam and Eve disobeyed His commandment: "Don't eat fruit from the tree that is in the middle of the Garden." As a result, the devil took over the right of ownership and used God's vessel to store his own product—sin. But don't forget this truth about the vessel: it was made to store God's product and nothing else.

*Now it is God who makes both us and you stand firm in Christ. He anointed us, set his seal of **ownership** on us, and put his Spirit in our hearts as a deposit, guaranteeing what is to come.*

2 Corinthians 1:21-22

Consider the above verses carefully. When the devil bought the right of ownership over man, he put his own product (evil spirits) inside the vessel (man). As a result, human beings could only produce sinful lives, because of the evil spirits placed inside them by Satan. This is the case with most people today.

People live sinful lives because of the evil spirits inside them. But when God bought back the right of ownership over man—through the death of His Son Jesus Christ—He emptied the devil's product (evil spirits) from the vessel (man) and restored to the vessel His own product (the Holy Spirit). He did this so that we could all live the righteous life that God had created us to live.

Through the blood of Jesus that was shed on the cross at Calvary, God bought back from the devil His right of ownership over man. Now, man should store God's product inside him, just as it was before he broke God's commandment. But unfortunately the eyes of most people are still blinded to this truth.

For you know that it was not with perishable things such as silver or gold that you were redeemed from the empty way of life handed to you from your forefathers, but with the precious blood of Christ, a lamb without blemish or defect.
1 Peter 1:18-19

Jesus Christ came to earth to free mankind from the devil's ownership. God the Father sent Him to free everyone from the devil's ownership over them.

How did Jesus Christ free mankind from the devil's ownership?

"Rabbi, we know you are a teacher who has come from God. For no one could perform the miraculous signs you are doing if God were not with him."
John 3:2

Listen carefully to Nicodemus' statement: "Rabbi, we know you are a teacher who has come from God." The question is, how did Nicodemus know that Jesus was from God? Because "no one could perform the miraculous signs you are doing if God were not with him." Nicodemus could tell that Jesus was no ordinary earthly being. How could he do that? Simply because he understood that earthly beings would not be able to do the miracles that Jesus was doing.

Nicodemus was saying to Jesus, "I can identify who you are; you are another type of being, simply because beings of this planet are not able to do the miracles you are doing." Are you getting that? Nicodemus could discern that Jesus' citizenship was not of this earth. He could see that Christ was from another planet, the planet of God.

In simple terms, Nicodemus was saying he was aware that Jesus was an alien from another planet—heaven. It was the miracles Christ was doing that brought this awareness to Nicodemus. That was the reason he said, *"No one could perform the miraculous signs you are doing unless he is from God."* No one on earth could do what Jesus was doing; therefore, for Him to be able to do what He was doing, He had to be from another planet!

Jesus understood very well what Nicodemus meant: that he was calling Him an alien from God's planet. He not only understood it, He loved it. What Jesus loved most was that this man was aware that He was not an earthly being but a heavenly one. Jesus loved the fact that Nicodemus could identify Him as being not of this world but of another place.

When you begin to understand what was going on in this dialogue, you will love it; this is one of the most interesting conversations you can ever read in the Bible.

Now let us look at Jesus' reply to Nicodemus:

"I tell you the truth, no one can see the kingdom of God unless he is born again."

John 3:3

What did Jesus mean by this statement? Remember that He understood very well what Nicodemus was saying, and He was responding to his calling Him an alien sent from God. What Jesus was saying was this: "You are right in saying that I am from God's planet; it is true that I am not an earthly being but a heavenly one." Jesus was agreeing with Nicodemus' statement that He was born of God's planet.

Listen very carefully again to Jesus' words: *"No one can see the kingdom of God unless he is born again."* What Jesus meant was that those miracles Nicodemus saw Him doing were a demonstration of how heaven actually operated. The miracles Jesus was doing on earth are normal in heaven (the kingdom of God, where He came from).

On earth, people called them "miracles" because they had never seen anything so amazing in their lives, since they were of the earth. But the things Jesus was doing on earth are normal activities in heaven; therefore they cannot be called "miracles" in heaven.

What Jesus wanted to tell Nicodemus was simply this: "Nobody can perform the miracles that I did, unless that person has been born into God's Kingdom—the same heavenly realm that I came from."

Born into God's Kingdom

Nicodemus could not understand what Jesus meant when He told him he needed to be "born again". Christ had said it was possible for Nicodemus to perform miracles too, if he were born into God's kingdom. For Nicodemus to do the same things Jesus was doing, he had to become a citizen of the heavenly kingdom.

"How can a man be born when he is old?" Nicodemus asked. "Surely he cannot enter a second time into his mother's womb to be born!"

John 3:4

Although Nicodemus could not understand the meaning of being born again, Jesus still loved his question. What Jesus loved about it was that Nicodemus understood this truth: to be born again, one had to come from another place into a new place. That was why he said, "Surely I cannot enter a second time into my mother's womb to be born."

We can understand Nicodemus' confusion. The word "again" means "for the second time"; so he thought that being "born again" meant having to go back into his mother's womb in order for her to give birth to him all over again. But what Jesus was talking about was Nicodemus regaining the originality that he had lost through Adam's fall.

Why did Jesus call it a "second-time" birth? Because, through the fall of Adam, man lost his first original birth. But, through the death and resurrection of Christ, God chose to give us another birth—this second birth that restores us to our former originality before Adam's fall. So what Jesus meant was that Nicodemus needed to be born into the realm of God, which was his true citizenship—not that he should return to his mother's womb, as he had thought.

The point Christ was making was that Nicodemus should regain his original birthright as a citizen of heaven, so that he too would be able to do the things that Jesus was doing—because the things that Jesus was doing were a demonstration of what man could do before the fall. Therefore, when we are born again, we regain our originality in Christ, and we are able to do the miracles that every citizen of heaven can do.

Born into the realm of Christ

Jesus went on to make it clear to Nicodemus that he was not talking about a second physical birth. In other words, Nicodemus did not need to enter his mother's womb a second time to be born again. What he needed to do was to come out of the kingdom of man (the earthly realm he had been living in) and enter into Christ's heavenly realm—the kingdom of God.

Jesus answered, "I tell you the truth, no one can enter the kingdom of God unless he is born of water and the Spirit."
John 3:5

People who live in the kingdom of God are very different from those who live in the kingdom of man. People who belong to the earthly realm are of the flesh, but people who belong to God's realm have His Spirit in them. Those who are of the flesh operate in the flesh; but those who are of God's Spirit operate in the Spirit.

This is what Christ was saying: "If you are born again into the kingdom of God, you can also do the miracles I am doing, because these things are done only by those who belong to God's kingdom." So, if Nicodemus desired to do the miracles Jesus was doing, he just needed to be born into Christ's realm, which is God's kingdom. Then he would be able to do all that Christ was doing.

To Jesus, the signs and wonders He was doing on earth were not miracles but merely the normal way things were done in His home country, heaven. Nothing Jesus did on earth was a surprise to Him, because He was just displaying the administration of

His native country, heaven. He raised the dead just to show us that there is no death in heaven. He changed water into wine to show us there is no poverty in heaven. He multiplied two fishes and five loaves to feed 5000 people, just to show us there is no lack in heaven.

All that Jesus did was done to demonstrate to us the administration of the kingdom of God. This was the same administration that Adam enjoyed before the fall. So all Christ did was to show the way in which Adam was supposed to be administering the earth, if not for the fall.

The flesh operates in a fleshly way, but the Spirit in a spiritual way

Flesh gives birth to flesh, but the Spirit gives birth to spirit.
John 3:6

This is the reason why people of the flesh—meaning people of this present world—do not understand those who have been born of the Spirit. Many times, they accuse Spirit-born people of using magical or even demonic powers to do what they do—more specifically, when they see these people performing miracles. Earthly people understand only how things work on earth. So it seems like magic to them when they see people of the Spirit demonstrating how things work in the heavenly realm. Born-again Christians are able to do the miracles that Christ did, simply because they have been born into the kingdom of God and are now displaying the administration of the heavenly realm, just like Christ did.

However, people out there in the world are not the only ones who have misconceptions about born-again believers. There are people in churches today who have not been born of the Spirit, and they think that being born again simply means becoming a member of a church. These people also join in to accuse Spirit-filled Christians of performing magic, especially when they see them healing the sick instantly and opening the eyes of the blind—not knowing that these are actually miracles that display the heavenly administration of Christ Jesus.

Since those who are truly born again have entered into God's kingdom, they are now able to display the administration of His kingdom. Like Christ, they now have citizenship in the heavenly realms, because they have been born into it. But many churches do not understand this, and some churches are even against those who perform miracles—simply because they still do not understand what it is to be born again.

When you get a revelation of what it means to be born again, you will begin to understand why those who are born again are able to perform miracles. It is because they are no longer earthly beings but heavenly beings through Christ Jesus. Actually, they do not consider what they do as miracles but simply demonstrations of what is normal in heaven.

Jesus also faced this problem during His time on earth. Because some people saw Him only as Joseph's son, they could not understand where His power came from. They accused Him of driving demons out with the help of Beelzebub, the prince of demons, because they could not understand that Christ was demonstrating the administration of the heavenly realm, where He came from.

Jesus was driving out a demon that was mute. When the demon left, the man who had been mute spoke, and the crowd was amazed. But some of them said, "By Beelzebub, the prince of demons, he is driving out demons."

Luke 11:14-15

We need to understand why some people accused Jesus of driving out demons with Beelzebub's help. They could not understand how Christ could do all that He did, since they regarded Him from a worldly point of view.

So from now on we regard no one from a worldly point of view. Though we once regarded Christ in this way, we do so no longer.

2 Corinthians 5:16

The Light of Life

It is the same with people who accuse born-again Christians of performing magic. They regard these miracle workers from a worldly point of view, just as they did with Christ. Such people do not understand that those who believe in Christ have crossed over from death to life.

"How can this be?" Nicodemus asked.

John 3:9

Nicodemus wanted to know how he could be born again; that was why he asked, "How can this be?" He was asking how it could be done, so that he could be freed from the devil's ownership. Listen to how Jesus responded to Nicodemus' question:

"Just as Moses lifted up the snake in the desert, so the Son of Man must be lifted up, that everyone who believes in him may have eternal life."

John 3:14-15

Remember that Jesus made this statement in reply to Nicodemus' question, "How can I be born again?" Now, what did He mean when He said that He "must be lifted up"? Why should He be lifted up?

The answer is that He was actually talking about His crucifixion, when He was "lifted up" on the cross. Through His blood shed on the cross, He bought back from the devil the right of ownership over man. Now everyone who believes in Jesus and receives Him as

Lord and Savior belongs to Him. They have been born again into the God's kingdom as His children.

Yet to all who received him, to those who believed in his name, he gave the right to become children of God—children born not of natural descent, nor of human decision or a husband's will, but born of God.

John 1:12-13

By leaving His place in heaven and coming to earth to die for our sins, Christ made a way for us to occupy His position in heaven. When He was lifted up on the cross, Jesus was leaving His position in heaven unoccupied, and He was also saying to the world, "Occupy my position so that, through it, you will take the citizenship of heaven, be saved from the devil's ownership, and become God's possession."

Therefore, all who believe in the name of Jesus have now taken Christ's position, which gives them the right to become children of God—because they have taken the position of the Son of God. They are no longer of the earth but are heavenly citizens in Christ. By taking Christ's position, we now have all the rights of children of God. It is my prayer that you will see the truth of all that I have said here, believe in the Lord Jesus, and take your rightful position as a child of God.

Reginald Nedzamba

Chapter 1

Your Life Belongs to God Your Maker

Your life is not yours, but belongs to the One who made you. You were not made for yourself but for God's purposes. This means the question you need to ask yourself is not "What do I want to do?" Rather, it should be "What was I made to do?" Why? Because you weren't created to fulfil your own goals but the goals of the One who made you.

If you don't agree with this statement and you say, "It's my life, I can do whatever I want with it," then allow me to ask you this question: *If your life truly belonged to you, why can't you stop yourself from dying when the time comes for you to die?* If you cannot refuse to die on the day of your death, this proves that your life is not within your control, but it is in the control of the One who made you.

You can't refuse to die when your time on earth is up; not even the best doctor can protect you on the day of your death. No one on this earth can keep you from dying when it is your time to die. Instead, when death comes for you, the doctor can do nothing except to watch in desperation as life leaves your body. No one can refuse to die when death comes calling—not even the richest, wisest or most powerful person who has ever lived. This shows that we do not have control over our lives. If we had, most people would refuse to die. Think about that.

All over the world, people are doing everything in their power to keep death at bay, but no one has ever succeeded. No scientist or doctor has ever come up with a prescription for immortality. No bodyguard has ever overcome the power of death. Princes and presidents have died in full view of their bodyguards; Death has stolen them away, even when they were guarded by the most fearsome protectors money could buy. Even those who claim there is no God are ultimately forced to surrender to a power greater than themselves—Death.

We have tried it all, and we have failed to overcome this enemy called Death. And I am willing to put my head on the block to say that nothing we can invent will *ever* be able to defeat the power of death. This is true as long as we are still on this earth, and it proves that our lives truly are not ours to control. It is clearly evident that Someone, somewhere, controls all our lives—whether we acknowledge or deny this fact. Our lives belong to the One who gave it to us.

This is the reason Jesus says you should not worry about your life. No matter how much you worry, it will not add an extra day or hour to your life. It does not matter how often you take your body to the doctor for a check-up. The check-up will not change God's appointed time for your death. In other words, you don't have any control over the time of your death. When you have to go—you have to go. It is not optional; it is obligatory. Have you ever thought of that? However, not every death happens at God's appointed time.

Our purpose is with God, not with us

Our lives on earth belong to God. Therefore we should allow Him to do whatever He has planned for us. Every life has a specific God-given purpose to fulfil on earth—and that purpose has nothing to do with us, but only with Him who made us. We are all created with a mission to accomplish here on earth.

"And now, compelled by the Spirit, I am going to Jerusalem, not knowing what will happen to me there. I only know that in every city the Holy Spirit warns me that prison and hardships are facing me.

"However, I consider my life worth nothing to me, if only I may finish the race and complete the task the Lord Jesus has given me—the task of testifying to the gospel of God's grace."

Acts 20: 22-24

I wept when I read Paul's declaration, "I consider my life worth nothing to me, if only I may finish the race and complete the task the Lord Jesus has given me." Certainly, the apostle made it vividly clear that his life had nothing to do with him. His only purpose on earth was to finish the task God had given him. Did you notice that? He said his life had nothing to do with his own task, but only God's task.

We too have been put on this earth to accomplish God's tasks, not our own. Your life is very important to God's mission here on earth. This is the reason you should not worry about your needs but only about finding the task God wants you to accomplish. If you don't fulfil that task, no one else will be able to do it. That should be scary because, on the Day of Judgment, all of us will be accountable to God for the tasks assigned to us.

You have been given a specific task that only you can fulfil. God has entrusted you—and you alone—with a mission no one else will be able to accomplish. Think about that for a while. There is something that is supposed to be done on this earth through you, and if our world misses out because you have not done it, you will be held accountable for that.

Every person born on this earth has been created for a specific purpose, to accomplish a particular mission in order for this world to take the shape God purposed it to take. And the failure of anyone to do his or her duty will affect the shape the world is supposed to take. Your absence from duty affects the direction this world takes. This means you are not only responsible for your family, spouse and children, but also for the affairs of the world.

Your purpose in life extends far beyond your own family and children. So, do not abdicate your responsibility to help shape the world—because you are going to have to stand before the judgment seat of God and answer for the duty He has assigned to you.

The world is like a company—God's company. It has many workers serving in different positions, but all with one purpose. We are all servants of God in this company called the world—and each one of us has a role to play, so that together we can take this world in the direction God wants it to go. And those who fail to do their duty will be held accountable on Judgment Day.

This is far more important than being able to say "I am a born-again Christian." It is not good enough just to be a born-again Christian, if you are not fulfilling your purpose on earth. Certainly, you need to be born again; but you also need to accomplish the task God has given you here on earth.

Every company has directors, managers, treasurers, secretaries, supervisors, workers, sales and marketing representatives, and human resource and security personnel. Every one of these employees is vitally important to the company, to help take it in the direction the Chairman wants it to go.

The Light of Life

The failure of anyone to perform his or her job affects the overall effectiveness and direction of the company. In fact, this is the very reason why you were employed—because, without you, the company will not be able to achieve its objectives. Furthermore, as part of the company, you do not work according to your own whims and fancies, but in the way the company requires of you— because you are working for the company and not yourself.

For this same reason, you have been placed on this earth: to work for the objectives of its Chairman, not your own. Imagine if one day an employee—say the office cleaner—doesn't arrive at work. What will happen? The workplace will be dirty, tea will not be served, the office staff will not be able to work as efficiently as they usually do, and this will affect the effectiveness and direction of the company. This means the office cleaner is not only responsible for his or her work, but also for the direction of the company. Imagine that!

So you should begin to understand how big your responsibility is. It is not about you and your family, but about the direction the world takes. You have an important role to play in steering the world in the direction God wants it to go. And if the company—that is, the world—misses the mark because you did not do your job, you will be held accountable on the Day of Judgment for dereliction of duty.

This is the reason God tells us that we should not worry about what we eat, drink or wear, but about our purpose on this earth. Don't live your life for pleasure but for your purpose, because nothing is worth more than accomplishing your purpose in life. You need to give careful thought to your purpose for living.

Most people live their lives only for themselves and their families, but your purpose in life extends far beyond yourself and your family. It is not just about you and your family, but about the whole world. It is very important to take care of your family, but your responsibility goes far beyond your family.

It is not about my church...*but about the world.*

It is not about my pastor...*but about the world.*

It is not about my ministry...*but about the world.*

It is not about my family...*but about the world.*

The Lord answered, "Who then is the faithful and wise manager, whom the master puts in charge of his servants to give them their food allowance at the proper time? It will be good for that servant whom the master finds doing so when he returns. I tell you the truth, he will put him in charge of all his possessions.

> *"But suppose the servant says to himself, 'My master is taking a long time in coming,' and he then begins to beat the menservants and maidservants and to eat and drink and get drunk. The master of that servant will come on a day when he does not expect him and at an hour he is not aware of. He will cut him to pieces and assign him a place with the unbelievers."*
>
> Luke 12:42-46

Jesus told this parable to illustrate the importance of doing your duty faithfully, so that you will earn a reward and not a rebuke from our Master when He returns. In the parable, the unfaithful manager neglected his responsibilities and started eating, drinking, and getting drunk. So my question to you is, "Are you doing what you were meant to do, or are you wasting the Master's time?" The answer is known only to you. But remember that you are put here on earth to perform a task, and there is no one else to do it but only you.

Let us look at the parable again: notice that the manager's duty was to give food to the menservants and maidservants, but instead he left the servants dying of hunger because he was too busy with his own business of getting drunk. Now my question to you is, "How many people here on earth are dying because you are not doing the task God appointed you to do?"

We will all be held accountable for deaths which weren't supposed to happen; they only happened because somebody neglected his or her duty. There are many bad things happening on earth, not because they are supposed to happen, but because those who are responsible for preventing them are not doing their job. And that person might be you.

Think about a security guard who is supposed to be on night duty, but fails to turn up for work. As a result, the building is left unguarded, and robbers break in and rob the company of its valuable assets. Who is responsible for that? Surely it is the security guard who is supposed to be at work, protecting the company's premises!

Now, think about yourself: are you on the job? Are you doing your God-given task? If you are not, how many things are going wrong on this earth because of your absence from work? So also you will be held accountable for some bad things that you could have prevented!

CHAPTER 2

It's not about the Gift but the Purpose of that Gift

Let us look at *Acts 20:22-24* again:

"And now, compelled by the Spirit, I am going to Jerusalem, not knowing what will happen to me there. I only know that in every city the Holy Spirit warns me that prison and hardships are facing me. However, I consider my life worth nothing to me, if only I may finish the race and complete the task the Lord Jesus has given me—the task of testifying to the gospel of God's grace."

Paul had been forewarned that, wherever he went, prison and hardships would be awaiting him. But he didn't care; his attitude was that, if prison and hardships were necessary to fulfil the task given to him by God, so be it. Why? Because Paul understood one thing: **Nothing, and I repeat, nothing on earth is more important than fulfilling the task God assigned to you.**

Nothing is worth more than completing the mission for which you were created. Everything has absolutely no value at all if you miss your mission—because your mission is the very reason you are here on earth. You can do a lot of good things in life but, if you don't complete God's given task for your life, you have achieved nothing.

Many people confuse their mission with their gifts; so, before we go any further, let me clarify that a gift and a mission are two different things. Most Christians find their gifts but never find the mission for their gifts. Actually, finding a gift is much easier than finding the mission that corresponds to the gift. A gift is not led by you, but a gift leads you; you don't direct your gift but your gift directs you. I hope you get my point. The mission (for which you were given the gift) does not lie in you yourself, but in God who gave you the gift.

Most churches on earth were established because of man's mission, not God's. In other words, it was man's idea, not God's, to establish those churches. And there are many other things that people do in God's name. But the truth is that it was man's idea, not God's, to do those things. People use God's name to make it look like it is God's mission, but in reality it is their own mission. The gift might be from God, but it is being used for their own mission. So it might seem to be God's mission, but in reality it is not God's mission; it is man's mission in God's name.

It is very vital that the gift given to you serves the right mission. This is because God has given you that gift for a specific mission—not for any mission. Most people serve the wrong mission with the right gift. When God gives you a gift, it is because He has already identified a specific mission for which that gift is required. And missing God's mission, for which the gift was given, is as bad as not having the gift. The gift belongs to God. It was given to you for God's specific mission; so you cannot use it for your own benefit, but only for God's benefit.

We are God's servants; this means we are serving God's business in the world, not our own. Therefore, we cannot do what we want with God's gift, but only what *He* wants—because the gift is His, not ours. Be careful that you do not serve your own purposes with God's gift.

The word of the LORD came to Jonah son of Amittai: "Go to the great city of Nineveh and preach against it, because its wickedness has come up before me."

Jonah 1:1

When God called Jonah, He didn't just call him. He also showed Jonah the mission He wanted him to accomplish—because, when God gave Jonah the gift of preaching, He had already identified the place (Nineveh) where Jonah's gift was required. However, most people just want to preach without a vision directing them to where their gift is required. Actually, most preachers won't establish a church in areas where people live in poverty, the reason being that they are not on God's mission but their own. They are in the business of making money through the church; this is man's idea, not God's.

And now I will show you the most excellent way. If I speak in the tongues of men and of angels, but have not love, I am only a resounding gong or a clanging cymbal. If I have the gift of prophecy and can fathom all mysteries and all knowledge, and if I have a faith that can move mountains, but have not love, I am nothing. If I give all I possess to the poor and surrender my body to the flames, but have not love, I gain nothing.

Love is patient, love is kind. It does not envy, it does not boast, it is not proud. It is not rude, it is not self-seeking, it is not easily angered, it keeps no record of wrongs. Love does not delight in evil but rejoices with the truth. It always protects, always trusts, always hopes, always perseveres.

Love never fails. But where there are prophecies, they will cease; where there are tongues, they will be stilled; where there is knowledge, it will pass away.

1 Corinthians 13:1-8

In the chapter preceding this (*1 Corinthians 12*), Paul was talking about spiritual gifts. Why then did he abruptly change the subject to love in Chapter 13? The answer is that, most of the time, the oft-quoted passage above has been misunderstood.

The love Paul was talking about is not the love that most of us think it is. Paul was actually talking about the purpose for which God gives you a gift. The gift is given to you, not to use in any way you wish, but in accordance with the mission of love for which it is given. This means it is not enough to say, "I've got a gift," but you need to find the mission for which the gift has been given.

Paul was actually saying that having a gift and using it for the wrong mission is meaningless. Preaching, prophesying and healing are not enough. You can move mountains with faith, but if you miss the purpose for that gift of faith, you have not done anything in the eyes of God. When you find a gift, you also have to find God's mission for that gift. It is not primarily important to have a gift, but it is essential to find the purpose of God for that gift.

Once you understand this, you will agree that most people serve their own missions with God's gifts. Paul said in *1 Corinthians 13:5* that love is not self-seeking. What did he mean by this? Simply that love does not seek to serve its own purposes or ideas, but seeks to serve God's mission. Most people, however, serve their own purposes using God's gifts. Actually, this is the problem with most Christians.

Love does not hastily serve any mission but is patient in finding its right and true mission, which is God's will as to how a particular gift is to be used. Few Christians find their true mission or are even aware that there is a specific mission for their gift.

It's not about the Gift but the Purpose of that Gift

Paul went on to say, a few verses later:

When I was a child, I talked like a child, I thought like a child, I reasoned like a child. When I became a man, I put childish ways behind me.
1 Corinthians 13:11

What Paul meant was that, when he was spiritually immature, he thought in a (spiritually) childish way—meaning that he thought the gifts of God were given to him to do with them what he himself desired. But when he had grown up spiritually, he began to realize that those gifts were given to him so that God's specific purposes could be accomplished. That was why Paul said he needed to fulfil the mission of love for which the gifts were given.

In other words, what Paul meant was that those who thought the gifts were given to them for their own use were still spiritual babies. But when they grew to spiritual maturity, they began to understand that the gifts of God were given to them so that they could accomplish God's specific tasks.

The verse above also tells us that there was a period in Paul's life when he was still a spiritual baby—when he thought God's gifts were given to him for any task of his own choice. He went on to say, "When I became a man, I put childish ways behind me." This means he no longer thought like a child— as he did before—but now he thought like a man.

When he became spiritually mature, he began to realize that the gifts he had been given were meant to fulfil God's specific purpose. So, too, our gifts are given to us to fulfil God's specific mission and not our own.

On the Day of Judgment, most people—including Christians—will be rejected. Not because they didn't do anything with their lives—no! But because they used the gifts of God for their own purposes and not God's purposes. It is therefore vitally important not to serve the wrong purposes with God's gifts; rather, we should find God's purpose for each gift. Jesus made it clear that he could reject even those who performed miracles, drove out demons, or prophesied in His name. This is not because the gift wasn't from God—no! The gift *was* from God, but it was used for the wrong purpose.

"Not everyone who says to me, 'Lord, Lord,' will enter the kingdom of heaven, but only he who does the will of my Father who is in heaven. Many will say to me on that day, 'Lord, Lord, did we not prophesy in your name, and in your name drive out demons and perform many miracles?'

"Then I will tell them plainly, 'I never knew you. Away from me, you evildoers!'"

Matthew 7:21-23

You see, it's not about driving out demons, performing miracles, or prophesying in His name; but it's about doing the will of God with the gifts He has given to us. The will of God is God's purpose for the gift He has given to you. You might have a gift; but, if you miss the purpose for which the gift was given, in the eyes of God you have failed.

Not only have you failed, you will also be rejected when you try to enter the kingdom of God on the Day of Judgment. It is not primarily important to be able to say, "I am a Pastor"… or "Bishop"… or "Apostle"… or "Prophet". But it is essential to find God's will—His purpose—for your gift.

CHAPTER 3

Not Your Will but His Will

Do you not know that your body is a temple of the Holy Spirit, who is in you, whom you have received from God? You are not your own.

1 Corinthians 6:19

When a company gives you a job, it expects you to fulfil its purposes, not your own. Isn't that true? Yes, of course! That's the reason for your employment. And, if the company realizes you are not fulfilling its purposes, it has the right to fire you—because you are not fulfilling what it has employed you for.

Similarly with our lives here on earth; if we are not fulfilling God's purposes, He has the right to fire us from His company (earth). Some people have died before their time because they were not doing God's will on earth. This is similar to a company firing you because you are not fulfilling the goals for which it hired you. So it is the same with some catastrophic deaths that have taken place on this earth.

Now there were some present at that time who told Jesus about the Galileans whose blood Pilate had mixed with their sacrifices. Jesus answered, "Do you think that these Galileans were worse sinners than all the other Galileans because they suffered this way? I tell you, no! But unless you repent, you too will all perish. Or those eighteen who died when the tower in Siloam fell on them—do you think they were more guilty than all the others living in Jerusalem? I tell you, no! But unless you repent, you too will all perish."

Luke 13:1-5

What is it that Jesus wants us to perceive here? It is this: there are people who die from catastrophes, not by accident, but because they are not fulfilling God's purposes on earth. Jesus gave us a warning: *"Unless you repent, you too will all perish."* If we do not repent and begin to live our lives for God, we have been warned that the same thing might happen to us; we might also perish before our time.

Don't get me wrong, I am not saying that God is killing people through calamities. What I am saying is that the eyes of God are not upon them to protect them when disaster strikes. Therefore they perish.

Then he told this parable: "A man had a fig tree, planted in his vineyard, and he went to look for fruit on it, but did not find any. So he said to the man who took care of the vineyard, 'For three years now I've been coming to look for fruit on this fig tree and haven't found any. Cut it down! Why should it use up the soil?'

"'Sir,' the man replied, 'leave it alone for one more year, and I'll dig around it and fertilize it. If it bears fruit next year, fine! If not, then cut it down.'"

Luke 13:6-9

When someone dies prematurely, the world asks, "Why did he die like that?" or "Was it his time to die?" The answer is that not all deaths happen because it is time for these people to die. No! This is not true at all. Actually, many premature deaths take place because most people are living for their own purposes and not for the purposes of their Creator. They are considered unworthy in the eyes of the Creator because they are not fulfilling the purposes for which He made them. God, the Creator and owner of the earth, allows people to die if He considers that they are not fulfilling His purposes on His earth.

WARNING!
If we are just eating, drinking, having pleasure, and fulfilling our own goals, we are in danger of being removed from this earth at any moment.

And he told them this parable: "The ground of a certain rich man produced a good crop. He thought to himself, 'What shall I do? I have no place to store my crops.'

"Then he said, 'This is what I'll do. I will tear down my barns and build bigger ones, and there I will store all my grain and my goods. And I'll say to myself, "You have plenty of good things laid up for many years. Take life easy; eat, drink, and be merry."'

"But God said to him, 'You fool! This very night your life will be demanded from you. Then who will get what you have prepared for yourself?'

"This is how it will be with anyone who stores up things for himself but is not rich toward God."
Luke 12:16-21

I encourage you to give this parable your full attention; did you hear what Jesus said? The first thing you need to note is this: the man hadn't yet done anything; he was just making plans. His life was taken away before he could begin to work out those plans. This shows us that our thoughts are observed by God the Father; so be careful what you plan to do, because it might be unworthy in God's eyes.

This parable also tells us that some people die because what they were planning to do on earth was unworthy in the eyes of the Creator. Most times we wonder and say, "What a good person! Why did he die like that?" But we don't know what the person was planning in his thoughts. Perhaps God knew his thoughts and said, "If you're planning to do that, you will not fulfil my purpose. Therefore your life will be taken from you."

The second thing we need to consider is this: this man thought that life was all about eating, drinking, and making merry. I am aware that most of us also have the same aspirations as him. We think:

❖ "If I can have a nice job, I've made it."

❖ "If I can have a nice house, I've made it."

THE LIGHT OF LIFE

- ❖ "If I can drive this kind of car, I've made it."

- ❖ "If I can have a successful business, I've made it."

- ❖ Or any other such thoughts.

Yes! You might have "made it" in your mind, but perhaps not in the mind of God your Maker. What you think of as "success" might not be success to Him. Therefore, if you fulfil your own desires but not His, you are not successful—because you are put on earth to fulfil His purposes and not your own.

"For my thoughts are not your thoughts, neither are your ways my ways," declares the LORD.

Isaiah 55:8

Most of us spend our lives pursuing our own desires and, in so doing, we end up missing God's will for us. This is because we have set our own thoughts above His thoughts. We occupy our minds with our own goals, and therefore we fail to achieve God's goals for our lives.

Our own goals have blocked us from perceiving God's goals for us; and this always results in our missing God's goals for our lives. In other words, your own goal has become an enemy to distract you and prevent you from finding God's goal for your life.

Most people's goals in life are to make money, get a nice house and car, and get married. These goals begin to control their lives, and they waste their time—which was supposed to be used to fulfil God's purposes—trying to fulfil their own dreams. Their goals have stolen their time and prevented them from achieving God's goals for them.

These people end up living for themselves, not for God. Their desires become their purpose for living, distracting them from fulfilling their true purpose in life. They are self-serving—servants of their own ambitions and not of God. They are driven by their own desires and not God's desires for them; and they live to fulfil their own purposes, not God's purposes. God's purposes are put on hold because these people are still striving to achieve their own ambitions.

True life

"Therefore I tell you, do not worry about your life, what you will eat or drink; or about your body, what you will wear. Is not life more important than food, and the body more important than clothes? Look at the birds of the air; they do not sow or reap or store away in barns, and yet your heavenly Father feeds them. Are you not much more valuable than they?"
Matthew 6:25-26

According to the Creator of life, your life is more important than eating, drinking, and looking good. In other words, your life has not reached its ultimate goal when you have acquired all the food, drinks and clothes you want. It is good to have these things, but these things are not life in themselves—these are the things you are given when you are living, not the things you should live for.

Most people work for things that are supposed to be given to them, not the things they should live for. Food, drinks and clothes are things that are supposed to be given to us. When you begin to fulfil God's purposes, your needs become God's responsibility. But when you live for your own purposes, your needs are your own responsibility. This is the reason most people live life trying to meet their own needs—because they live life for their own purposes. Therefore God does not supply their needs.

To illustrate: most people think that the purpose of working for their employer is to get an income. But that is not the truth. The main purpose of your working for your employer is to serve the needs of the employer—to fulfil the purposes for which the company has hired you. You are not in the company just to consume the company's money to buy things for yourself. First and foremost, you are in the company to fulfil the purposes for which the company has hired you. Then the company will make sure that you get an income to live on. In other words, you are not working for your income, but for the success of the company.

This means that being in the company is more important than getting your income. Therefore, you can now understand why being on earth is more important than eating, drinking and wearing clothes. We are on earth to fulfil the purposes of the One who owns this company called Earth. We are to seek first to fulfil His purposes, and in turn He will fulfil our needs—food, clothes, car, house, and so on.

"So do not worry, saying, 'What shall we eat?' or "What shall we drink?' or 'What shall we wear?' For the pagans run after all these things, and your heavenly Father knows that you need them. But seek first his kingdom and his righteousness, and all these things will be given to you as well. Therefore do not worry about tomorrow, for tomorrow will worry about itself. Each day has enough trouble of its own."

Matthew 6:31-34

Fulfil the tasks your employer has set you, and your salary becomes his responsibility. Most people are worried about a responsibility that is not theirs to worry about. Your salary is not something you should worry about; you should only be worried about doing the job which your employer (God) has hired you to do. Then, it becomes your employer's responsibility to pay you. Therefore, do not worry about what you will eat, drink or wear; the only thing to worry about is doing your work. Your salary is not your responsibility; it is your employer's responsibility.

I once hired a house cleaner to clean a newly-built house that was very dirty. I showed him what I wanted him to do, and we agreed on the price I would pay when he had completed the work. One thing I learned from this worker: he never once asked me about his wages, but I was the one who had to worry about the payment for his labour. He did his work as I had instructed him, and I was pleased with the way he went about it. And, even before he told me he had finished the job, I already had his wages in my pocket—ready to pay him.

The house cleaner knew his responsibility—to complete the task for which I had hired him. And my responsibility was to make sure that he got paid. So it is the same with our relationship with God: we do the tasks God has given us on earth, and He makes sure we get all we need. Your responsibility is to complete God's work according to His will, not to worry about your income—that is God's responsibility. And He already has your wages in His pocket—ready to pay you once you have successfully completed your job.

Look at the birds of the air

"Look at the birds of the air; they do not sow or reap or store away in barns, and yet your heavenly Father feeds them. Are you not much more valuable than they?"

Matthew 6:26

Birds can teach us what life is all about. They were born to fly in the sky. This is the purpose for which they were created, and they accomplish it all the time. But when they get hungry, they come back to the ground to find food. And there is food waiting for them—although they don't grow or store it. Why? Because birds fulfil the purpose for which they were made; therefore God provides for all their needs.

What I have learnt from birds

At home, we get our water from a bore hole, pumping it from the hole with an electric motor. One day I was sitting under a tree, watching as my young sister pumped up the water. I realized that the pipe which transported water from the bore hole was leaking and some of the water was flowing out of the leaking pipe into a small gully next to it. Within five or ten minutes, a couple of birds had alighted and started to drink the water and bathe in it.

Then the Holy Spirit spoke to me, "Do you see something? The pipe is leaking, but it isn't accidental. It is so that these birds can come to drink and even bathe in the water leaking from the pipe."

Then I started to think about what Jesus had said, "Look at the birds… they do not sow or reap… and yet your heavenly Father feeds them. Are you not much more valuable than they?"

The Light of Life

What was God's purpose in creating us?

Then God said, "Let us make man in our image, in our likeness, and let them rule over the fish of the sea and the birds of the air, over the livestock, over all the earth, and over all the creatures that move along the ground."

So God created man in his own image, in the image of God he created him; male and female he created them.

God blessed them and said to them, "Be fruitful and increase in number; fill the earth and subdue it. Rule over the fish of the sea and the birds of the air and over every living creature that moves on the ground."

Genesis 1:26-28

The Scripture passage above reveals the plan God had in mind when He created us. The most important thing to understand is that, when God created the heavens and the earth, His intention was to see both of them functioning in exactly the same way. God began by creating the heavens and then, after creating the heavens, He created the earth. But what we need to know is that God created the earth as a branch (in other words, a regional division) of heaven. By creating the earth as a branch, God intended it to function like heaven.

In the beginning God created the heavens and the earth. Now the earth was formless and empty, darkness was over the surface of the deep, and the Spirit of God was hovering over the waters.

Genesis 1:1-2

When God first created the earth, it was empty and in darkness because there was nothing in it yet—it was still under construction. But, after establishing it as a branch of heaven, God started placing on the earth all the things it would need in order to function like heaven. Keep in mind the picture that this earth was made as a branch of heaven; therefore, whatever God placed on it was created as a replica of something that could already be found in heaven.

Suppose you and I purchased the same type of phone; we would expect both our phones to function in exactly the same way. We would have the same service from our phones because they would both have the same functions and be the same in every way. Both our phones would function equally well; and the secret behind their identical functionality would lie in the circuitry the manufacturer had placed inside them.

Or consider this illustration: we have McDonald's in South Africa and MacDonald's in USA, and the restaurants in both of these countries offer the same service and quality. Therefore they are similar. But there exists someone what we will call "McDonald the Father"—the owner of the first McDonald's restaurant. "McDonald the Father" was the one who shared his know-how (knowledge) with the other McDonald's restaurant owners all over the world.

Therefore they all function in the same way because they share the same know-how (knowledge). So it is with us and God the Father. God the Father offers His service in heaven, while we offer ours on earth.

What you find at McDonald's USA, you will also find at McDonald's in South Africa. The reason behind their identical service and quality is that they share the same know-how (knowledge). But, if it so happens that one of them loses this knowledge, it will not be able to maintain the same high standards as before—because the key to its service and quality lies in the knowledge it used to possess but has lost.

Now, here is the truth: when God created human beings, He created them to be exactly like Himself. God wanted man to function just like Himself; in other words, we were made to provide the earth with exactly the same quality of service that God provides in heaven. Heaven looks the way it looks because of the service God offers to it. Therefore, in order for the earth to receive the same service as heaven, God had to replicate Himself in man.

This is the purpose for which you and I were put on earth. God's intention was that whatever He did in heaven would be done on earth through His replica, man. He deposited His own know-how (knowledge) into His replica (man), so that man would do on earth what He was doing in heaven.

The interruption of God's original plan

Then God said, "Let us make man in our image, in our likeness..." So God created man in his own image, in the image of God he created him; male and female he created them.

Genesis 1:26-27

God created us in His own image, so that we would be exactly like Him. This means that, after God created man, He looked at him and said, "Wow, I've created a copy of myself—this is me!"

When God created man, he made him in the likeness of God.

Genesis 5:1

When God duplicated Himself in man, He was very sure that all He did in heaven would be done on earth through man. In other words, God approved man as "god" on earth. This means God placed in man all that was within him in order for man to function as God on earth—to do all that God could do. All the know-how (knowledge) of God was put inside man. In other words, man was like God because God shared all His knowledge with him.

You will recall that the similarity between McDonald's in the USA and McDonald's in South Africa is the knowledge that they both share. The first McDonald's to be established (by McDonald the Father) shared their trade secrets (knowledge) with another branch and approved it as a McDonald's restaurant too. Why? Because these trade secrets (knowledge) were deposited in McDonald the branch, in the same way that God had deposited His knowledge in man. What makes a place a McDonald's restaurant is not the building where it is housed, but the know-how (knowledge) that is being used in the building to prepare and serve food the McDonald's way.

Here is another illustration: you find a recipe (knowledge) in a magazine for a cake you have always wanted to learn to bake. But when you are about to make the cake, you realize you have lost the magazine. Will you be able to proceed with the cake? The answer is No! Why not? Because you have lost the recipe (knowledge) telling you how to do it. In other words, by losing the recipe (knowledge) you have actually lost your cake.

The devil knew very well that man was not God, but the knowledge that was within man made him function like God. The devil also knew that, to destroy the likeness of God in man, he had to destroy the knowledge that God had placed in man. And that was exactly what he did—by replacing the knowledge from God with another kind of knowledge.

This was how it happened: after God created man He gave him a warning…

*"You are free to eat from any tree in the garden; but you must not eat from the tree of the **knowledge** of good and evil, for when you eat of it you will surely die."*
Genesis 2:16-17

God was trying to communicate something very important to man through this warning. Notice that He used the word "**knowledge**" here; what He was saying to man was this: "The secret behind our likeness lies in the **knowledge** I have shared with you, so please protect my **knowledge,** which is within you." Man had been warned by God not to eat fruit from the tree which was in the middle of the garden; for God had said to man, "When you eat of it you will surely die."

Did man fall down and die physically after eating fruit from the tree? No! Was God lying? Definitely not! So what kind of death was God talking about? It was the death of God's likeness in man.

God was saying that the tree in the middle of the garden contained the **knowledge** of good and evil. Therefore, if man ate from it, he would receive within himself the **knowledge** of good and evil; and that would replace the **knowledge** God had already shared with him—the knowledge that made man to be like God.

In other words, what God was telling man was this: "If you eat from that tree, you will die (that is, the likeness of God in you will die), and you will become a man knowing both good and evil, as a result of the **knowledge** contained in that tree." The devil knew all this; so he tricked man into disobeying God and eating from the tree of the knowledge of good and evil:

Now the serpent was more crafty than any of the wild animals the LORD *God had made. He said to the woman, "Did God really say, 'You must not eat from any tree in the garden'?"*

The woman said to the serpent, "We may eat fruit from the trees in the garden, but God did say, 'You must not eat fruit from the tree that is in the middle of the garden, and you must not touch it, or you will die.'"

"You will not surely die," the serpent said to the woman. "For God knows that when you eat of it your eyes will be opened, and you will be like God, knowing good and evil."

When the woman saw that the fruit of the tree was good for food and pleasing to the eye, and also desirable for gaining wisdom, she took some and ate it. She also gave some to her husband, who was with her, and he ate it.

Genesis 3:1-6

Man ate from the tree and, as a result, he died—the likeness of God in man was erased, replaced by the knowledge of good and evil. This is why there is both good and evil in human beings right up to this day.

Chapter 4

The Restoration of God's Original Plan

The first thing God the Father wanted to do when He sent Christ to earth was to display the true life of man through His Son. In other words, Jesus' life on earth was an example of how man's life was supposed to be lived, if not for the fall.

The way we live now is not how we were originally created to live. We are not living as our true selves now—because we are not living the life that God originally designed us to live, but we are living the life which came to us as a result of man's fall in the Garden of Eden. So the life we live now is not the life that was originally intended for us.

The life that I live now is not my true life, but evil is living within me. This is because I lost my true life in the Garden of Eden, when man disobeyed God. That was why Jesus said, *"I am the way and the truth and the life." (John 14:6)*. The life Jesus lived on earth demonstrated the true life of man before the fall. So, when we look at Jesus' life, we actually see our true lives—the lives we would have lived if not for the fall.

When you see someone robbing or killing another person, understand this: it is not him, but sin or evil doing it through him. Similarly, when we hear people saying, "I'm a gay" or "I'm a lesbian"; they are not their true selves, but they are what they are because of the fall.

Do you know why people are homosexuals? Perhaps you have friends, acquaintances or relatives who are gays or lesbians, or you yourself may be homosexual too. And you may be asking, "Why do they feel like this?" (Or "Why do I feel this way?") I have an answer for you: that feeling is not truly theirs (or yours), but stems from the knowledge of good and evil living inside human beings as a result of the disobedience of Adam. In other words, it is not the real them (or you), but sin or evil living inside them (or you).

Homosexuals get criticized by others for being the way they are. But how can anyone criticize them? They didn't choose to feel that way; they were born with those feelings. Sometimes even Christians do not want homosexuals near them. But let me tell you something: God wants them near Him. He knows what they are going through. God understands their feelings. Actually, that is the reason He sent Jesus Christ to the earth: Jesus came to resolve all our situations and restore us to our true selves.

Christ Jesus came to the earth for the unhealthy. This includes gays and lesbians, because being a gay or a lesbian is unhealthy. Most churches run away from the very issues that Jesus came to earth to resolve, because most churches still do not understand the significance of the church.

While Jesus was having dinner at Matthew's house, many tax collectors and "sinners" came and ate with him and his disciples. When the Pharisees saw this, they asked his disciples, "Why does your teacher eat with tax collectors and 'sinners'?"

On hearing this, Jesus said, "It is not the healthy who need a doctor, but the sick."

Matthew 9:10-12

The reason Jesus came to the earth was to heal the world's sicknesses. But what amazes me is that most churches run away from the very same things that Jesus came to heal. If Jesus came to heal adulterers, how can the church run away from them? If Jesus came to heal corrupt people, how can the church run away from them? If Christ came to heal homosexuals, how can the church of Jesus Christ run away from them? This can only be done by a church that doesn't belong to Christ but to its own members.

The church of Jesus Christ is here on earth to be a solution to the problems of this world, but most churches love only those who are spiritually healthy. Christ came to be a doctor to the sick—that means all of us. Our symptoms are not the same, but we are all corrupted. This is the reason we need to be born again—because our first birth was corrupted by sin through the deception of the devil. Being gay is one of the symptoms of the first corrupted man, Adam.

We need to be refabricated, because the first fabrication was corrupted. Because man was corrupted by the devil in the Garden of Eden, we all need to be born again.

I am not myself but sin lives in me

We know that the law is spiritual; but I am unspiritual, sold as a slave to sin. I do not understand what I do. For what I want to do I do not do, but what I hate I do. And if I do what I do not want to do, I agree that the law is good. As it is, it is no longer I myself who do it, but it is sin living in me.

I know that nothing good lives in me, that is, in my sinful nature. For I have the desire to do what is good, but I cannot carry it out. For what I do is not the good I want to do; no, the evil I do not want to do—this I keep on doing.

Now if I do what I do not want to do, it is no longer I who do it, but it is sin living in me that does it.

Romans 7:14-20

My father ran a taxi business, and I grew up repairing taxis with him. This experience has given me a better understanding of *Romans 7:14-20*. I recall the day when one of the taxis broke down. It could start, but it couldn't move. So I asked my dad what was wrong with the taxi, and he replied, "It's the clutch plate."

This really shocked me, so I asked my father if this thing called a clutch plate was what had caused the car to break down; and my dad said, "Yes, it is only the clutch plate."

What I learned from this experience was that, though there was nothing wrong with the car's body, it couldn't go anywhere simply because the clutch plate was damaged. In other words, the faulty clutch plate had caused the whole car to stop working—although everything else about the car was fine. The clutch plate problem was affecting the whole taxi. Every malfunction in the car was a symptom of one thing called a clutch plate. All that my father and I needed to do was to replace the defective clutch plate, and every symptom in the car would disappear.

Imagine what would have happened if we had given this car to someone who didn't know what the problem was—he wouldn't have known what to do. He might even have caused more problems to the car because he might have worked on things that weren't the cause of the problem.

In the same way, everything amiss in our lives is caused by one thing called sin. Sicknesses of body and mind, criminal behaviour, adultery, corruption, in fact whatever goes wrong in or with human beings—all are caused by one thing called sin living in man.

They are all symptoms of the sin in man. Let me clarify this:

- ❖ Crime is not sin in itself;
- ❖ Adultery is not sin in itself;
- ❖ Corruption is not sin in itself.

All of the above are the fruit of the tree called sin. Therefore, if you remove the tree (sin) in man, you will also remove the fruit of the tree. But if you fight the symptoms (the fruit), you will not win the fight because you are not tackling the true problem (the tree). This is what doctors, psychologists, social workers, community leaders, the police, and everyone else are doing—they are not fighting the real problem but the symptoms of the problem. This is because they do not understand that all these are the fruit of sin. God alone knows man's real problem and the solution to the problem.

The Book of Romans was written by Paul. He discovered that the man living inside him was not his true self, but it was sin living in him, because he was a fallen man. He said in *Romans 7:14*, "We know that the law is spiritual; but I am unspiritual, sold as a slave to sin." What did he mean by that?

What he was saying was this: "Through Adam's sin (eating from the forbidden tree), I have been sold as a slave to sin. The life I was originally meant to live was spiritual, but man's fall (through Adam's disobedience) has transformed my spiritual life into an unspiritual life. Adam's disobedience transformed my being. Therefore, the law of God speaks about who I was before the fall—the law speaks about the type of man I was intended to be (before the fall). I wasn't made to be covetous; I wasn't made to be a thief; I wasn't made to be an adulterer; I wasn't made to be a gay; I wasn't made to be a prostitute; I wasn't made to be a robber.

"But the problem is that, I lost my righteous life when I lost my true life through Adam's disobedience. Therefore, what the law says I should do, I can't do. I can't live my true life, because the sinful life has replaced my righteous life—which I could have lived, if not for the fall. So I (the spiritual man) have disappeared, but sin (the unspiritual man) lives in me."

As it is, it is no longer I myself who do it, but it is sin living in me.
Romans 7:17

Suppose you purchased a car with a manual (the law of the car). All the functions of the car are listed in the manual (the law). Now, suppose the manual tells you that, when you turn the key, the car will start. But, when you turn the key, the car doesn't respond.

But the manual (the law) says the car *must* start when you turn the key! Now, where do you think the problem lies? Could it be that something is wrong with car? Or is the manual (the law) lying? Which is wrong? The car or the manual?

The truth is, the manual can never be wrong about its product (the car). So, there must be something wrong with the product itself. The manual reveals the true functionality of the product. If the product does not do what the manual says, it means that something is wrong with the product, not the manual.

So it is with the law (the manual) of God regarding man (the product). The law speaks of who we really are. But we are unable to live according to the law of God! Why? Because there is something wrong with us—sin has replaced our true life. Therefore, we are unable to live according to the law of God. We need to be repaired and restored to our original good condition before the fall, so that we can live according to God's law. This is why God sent Christ to the earth—to repair us so that we can regain our original functionality.

Here is another illustration of the same truth: suppose you were a prostitute—of course, you would know that you were a prostitute but, if someone called you a prostitute, would you like it? The truth is No! You wouldn't like it. Why so? Because, even though you were a prostitute, you didn't like what you did. If you liked what you did, you wouldn't be angry when someone called you a prostitute. But the reason you got angry is that you didn't like what you did. Therefore, if you didn't like what you did, it means you agree that prostituting is not right—though you might have kept on doing it.

If you don't like what you do but keep on doing it, it means that it is not the real you who is the one doing it. Rather, it is sin or evil that is doing it through your body. You cannot help yourself, but you do it even though you don't like to do it. This means you are someone's slave—you are a slave to sin, because sin forces you to do things you don't want to do. Therefore, it is not you who is the one doing it, but it is sin that is living in you.

Let us look at another example: women who engage in casual sex, get pregnant, and end up aborting or abandoning their babies. They do things that cause them to become pregnant, but when the babies come along, they don't want them. This means they agree that they weren't supposed to become pregnant. This means they agree that it was not their own choice to be pregnant. Whose choice was it then?

It is ridiculous, isn't it? How can you do things that will get you pregnant but, when you get pregnant, you don't want the baby? It doesn't make sense, does it? This again proves that it was not their decision to get pregnant, but sin made them do it. If it really was their own decision, they would not have reversed it by aborting or abandoning their babies. The fact that they did so is proof that they were not the ones who made the decision to get pregnant; something else—the sin in them—made that decision for them.

To conclude: when people do a wrongful thing, it is not really they themselves who are doing it, but it is the sin in them that does it through them. And no one in this world will be able to solve this problem of sinful man—except the One who created man and who knows where the problem lies.

Even our laws prove the law has failed

In most countries, there are laws against murder, assault, robbery, rape, cheating, corruption and other criminal activities. But, although the law may tell us not to murder or rob, murders and robberies still take place. The law may tell us not to rape, but the raping still goes on. The law may tell us not to engage in corrupt practices, but corruption still abounds. All this goes to show that the law does not have the solution to these problems. I mean, even the very people who enacted these laws have broken them. They are still corrupt.

The law says, "Don't rape anyone; if you do, you will go to prison for many years." However, the prisons are still getting full because, although people know the penalty for rape, they can't stop themselves from doing it. Not because they want to go to prison, but because they can't help themselves; it is the sin in them that is making them do it. Nobody really knows where the problem is, so we think that they are doing it intentionally. However, the truth is that it is not their true selves doing it, but sin is doing it through them.

In some countries, they cut off people's hands for stealing. But even the threat of such a severe punishment does not stop the thieves. Not because they like to have their hands chopped off, but because they cannot help themselves. It is not their true selves doing it, but it is sin doing it through them.

Some countries impose the death penalty for murder; but still that doesn't stop people from killing each other. Not because they like to die, but because they were not their true selves when they killed the other person. It was sin doing it through them. This is the reason some murderers say, "I wish I hadn't done it." If they had truly wanted to do it, they would not have regretted it. The fact that they regretted doing it shows that it wasn't their intention to commit the crime, but something else—sin—did it through them.

You may be asking, "How about those people who have never committed any crime?" Does that mean there is no sin in them? No, not at all! It simply means that their sins are not as obvious as those of others. The truth is that we are all sinners, and we know it. If our sins were punishable under the law, we would have been arrested many times by now.

Many sins are not punishable offences under the law; if they were, most people would be serving time in jail by now. Think, for instance, about the sin of adultery: how many more people would have been arrested, if one had to go to prison for adultery? And there are many other sins that are not punishable under the law.

And, think about this too: there are no degrees of sin in God's eyes. All sins are equal in His eyes. An adulterer is just as guilty in God's eyes as a murderer.

The whole world is full of sinners—it is simply that we don't all commit the same sin. Some of us commit sins that make us more notorious than others. However, in God's eyes, we are all sinners and we all deserve the same punishment.

The teachers of the law and the Pharisees brought in a woman caught in adultery. They made her stand before the group and said to Jesus, "Teacher, this woman was caught in the act of adultery. In the Law Moses commanded us to stone such women. Now what do you say?"

They were using this question as a trap, in order to have a basis for accusing him. But Jesus bent down and started to write on the ground with his finger.

When they kept on questioning him, he straightened up and said to them, "If any one of you is without sin, let him be the first to throw a stone at her." Again he stooped down and wrote on the ground.

At this, those who heard began to go away one at a time, the older ones first, until only Jesus was left, with the woman still standing there.

John 8:3-9

Consider Jesus' wisdom in dealing with the situation. He knew that all had sinned, each in his own way. He knew that all those people accusing the woman of adultery had sins of their own too. It could be that their sins were different from the woman's; but the fact remained that they were all sinners as well.

The teachers of the law and the Pharisees, together with the people, thought that the woman deserved to be judged for her sin, but not they for theirs. Jesus made them aware that the woman's sin and theirs were judged as equal in the eyes of God.

Why did they leave after Jesus spoke to them? Because Jesus' statement brought consciousness to the people of their own sins. They left the woman alone because every one of them was now conscious of his own sin. This was the reason they left Jesus alone with the woman.

So it is with the whole world; it is full of sinners. Our sins might not be the same, but the fact is that we are all sinners:

- ❖ The police who arrest people are conscious of their own sins;

- ❖ Traffic officers who hand out tickets to people are conscious of their own sins;

- ❖ Magistrates who mete out judgments to people are conscious of their own sins;

- ❖ Government leaders who enact laws for their countries are also conscious of their own sins.

With man, there are degrees of sin; but it is not so with God. With God, all sins are equal and deserve the same punishment. Therefore, we should understand that the sins which put people in prison and those which do not are, in the eyes of God, all equally deserving of the same punishment.

If you steal but you don't kill, the sin of stealing is just as bad as the sin of killing in the eyes of God. If you don't kill but you commit adultery, in God's eyes you are just as guilty as those who kill; and therefore you deserve the same punishment as them. In God's eyes, we are all sinners, "for all have sinned and fall short of the glory of God" (*Romans 3:23*).

The Restoration of God's Original Plan

Now if I do what I do not want to do, it is no longer I who do it, but it is sin living in me that does it.
Romans 7:20

We inherited this evil nature—the sin living in us—from the first man, Adam. This means man is no longer the product God created him to be before the fall. Governments can enact the best laws on earth but, until the product (man) is repaired, these laws will not work. People will always break the law because the problem is with the product itself, not with the laws governing the product.

Governments are also aware of this fact, though they may not see it that way. Look at this interesting example: at first, when dealing with the spread of HIV, the government in some countries decreed that people must abstain from casual sex and only have sex with their regular partners. However, that didn't stop people from being unfaithful to their partners and continuing to have sex with multiple partners. As a result, the rate of HIV infections continued to grow.

So these countries came up with another strategy, that of giving condoms to the people. Why did the government in these countries decide to give out condoms? Because they had tried the first strategy of using the law to get people to abstain from casual sex, but they came to realize that it didn't work. Although people knew the law, they didn't practise it.

By providing condoms, these countries were tacitly admitting that their laws had failed to stop people from engaging in casual sex. Not that they condoned people having multiple sex partners, No! The point is that they were supplying condoms not out of choice but necessity. If the law had been able to get people to do what they should, governments would not have had to give out condoms; but giving out condoms showed that the law had failed.

In other words, government leaders are aware that whatever law they try to implement, it does not rectify the life of man. This means they agree with what God has been telling us all along: that the law cannot make man righteous, because man is corrupt. Man needs to be refabricated (born again). And God wants to refabricate us into a new creation through Christ Jesus. As it says in the Bible:

Therefore, if anyone is in Christ, he is a new creation; the old has gone, the new has come!

2 Corinthians 5:17

How God resolved the problem of sin

Man was originally created in the image of God but, when the devil tricked him into eating the forbidden fruit, this image of God died in man. In other words, the devil killed the true life of man through his trickery. Man died to his true self, and God's plan for him was destroyed. This was how the devil destroyed God's plan for mankind and raised up his own plan. But God turned the tables on the devil by destroying sin in man through the death of Christ.

When Christ died, sinful man died too, because Christ died for him. And Christ did not just die to destroy sin, He rose again to restore man to his true self and life. The devil had tried to destroy God's plan for mankind through deceiving one man: Adam. But God destroyed the devil's plan by raising back to life His original plan for mankind, through the resurrection of one Man: Christ Jesus.

For just as through the disobedience of the one man the many were made sinners, so also through the obedience of one man the many will be made righteousness.
Romans 5:19

Psychiatrists may prescribe treatment for deviant behaviour. Governments may enact all kinds of laws to curb crime. All these do not work because the product called man was damaged long ago in the Garden of Eden. Governments, social workers, psychiatrists and psychologists are all unable to fix the problem. Only God knows where man's problem lies and how to solve it.

God knew that the only solution was to replace the damaged product with a new one. And He did exactly that, by crucifying you and me on the cross through Christ Jesus. God destroyed every one of us on the cross—because He knew that man's problem was sin living in him, and the only way to solve this problem was to destroy him and refabricate him.

Through the death and resurrection of Jesus Christ, God has done just that; He has destroyed the corrupted product and refabricated it through one Man, Christ Jesus. This is the reason we say, "We are born again." We are no longer a corrupted creation, but a new creation refabricated through Christ Jesus.

Therefore, when Christ was crucified on the cross and buried, every sinful man died with Him because He died for them. By crucifying Jesus on the cross, God was demonstrating to the world that sinful man is now dead and gone. By raising Jesus from the dead, God was also demonstrating to the world that the man God originally created (and whom the devil destroyed in Eden) has now been restored to life.

So the death of Christ symbolizes the death of the corrupted man, Adam. And the resurrection of Jesus Christ symbolizes the restoration of the righteous man on earth.

CHAPTER 5

You Cannot Serve Both the Spirit and the Flesh

Then Jesus said to his disciples: "Therefore I tell you, do not worry about your life, what you will eat; or about your body, what you will wear."

Luke 12:22

Jesus told His disciples not to think of the needs of the body. Why not? Because He did not want them to live life to fulfill the needs of the flesh and thereby miss the needs of the spirit. Man was not created to live for the flesh. The body is designed to be a vessel to hold the Manufacturer's product—that is, the Spirit. Therefore the product (the Spirit) does not live for the vessel (the body) but the vessel lives for the product.

Or to put it another way: the body is the truck that carries the product (the Spirit) to where it is supposed to go. The duty of the truck is to deliver the product to its destination. The needs of the truck are not the responsibility of the truck itself, but of the product's manufacturer. If the truck needs fuel, new tires, brake fluid, oil, water or servicing, it is the manufacturer of the product who will take care of these needs, not the truck itself. The manufacturer knows that, if the truck is not properly looked after, it will fail to deliver the product. Therefore the manufacturer makes sure that all the needs of the truck are met, so that it will succeed in delivering the product to its destination.

So it is with us: the body is the vehicle that should deliver the Spirit (the product) to its destiny. God is the Manufacturer of the product; therefore, He is responsible for looking after the needs of the vehicle (the body), so that it can successfully deliver the product (the Spirit) to its destiny. This is why Jesus tells us not to think of the needs of the body; because He (the Manufacturer) will look after them.

Just imagine, if the truck existed only to meet its own needs—to get fuel, new tires, brake fluid, oil, water and servicing for itself—what do you think will happen? It will fail to deliver the product, because it is only meeting its own needs instead of the needs of the manufacturer. Similarly, when we live life for our own selfish ends, we will never fulfill our purpose, because we are being driven by our own needs instead of the purpose of the Manufacturer.

The true function of the mind

The mind was never designed to think the thoughts of the flesh. If it does that, it will misdirect the product (the Spirit) to the wrong destiny—the selfish desires of the flesh. When you keep thinking of the needs of the flesh, you allow the flesh to direct your life—which means you will not deliver the product (the Spirit) to its right destiny, because you have another destination in mind, that of the flesh. Instead of delivering the Spirit to its rightful destiny, you deliver it to the destination directed by your flesh. To avoid this, you have to stop thinking of your physical needs.

Using the mind to mind the flesh is mind abuse, because our minds were never designed to mind our flesh but only the Spirit. We are not supposed to mind the flesh; that is not the true function of the mind. The mind's true function is to receive the vision (purpose) from the Spirit and communicate it to the body, and then the body can begin to live out that vision. In this way, the body is serving the Spirit, which is its true purpose. This is how we are supposed to discover our purpose on earth—by receiving through our minds the vision (purpose) from the Spirit. Man's purpose on earth is hidden within the Spirit.

No one can tell you your purpose on earth except the Spirit within you. As you act out what is being communicated from the Spirit to your mind, you will begin to discover your purpose in life. Note, too, that the Spirit does not communicate everything to you at once. He takes you step by step; as you obey the first step, you will be given the next step, and the next step will take you to another step, until you reach your full destiny. In other words, you cannot have the full vision of your purpose all at once, but you unfold it step by step as you act out the Spirit's instructions.

And he told them this parable: "The ground of a certain rich man produced a good crop. He thought to himself, 'What shall I do? I have no place to store my crops.'

"Then he said, 'This is what I'll do. I will tear down my barns and build bigger ones, and there I will store all my grain and my goods. And I'll say to myself, "You have plenty of good things laid up for many years. Take life easy; eat, drink and be merry."

"But God said to him, 'You fool! This very night your life will be demanded from you. Then who will get what you have prepared for yourself?'

"This is how it will be with anyone who stores up things for himself but is not rich toward God."

Luke 12:16-21

Where did this man go wrong, that his life should be demanded from him? This was what he did wrong: *he thought to himself.* He was using his mind to think of self, which is misusing the mind. His mind was being used to think of himself. Therefore, if his mind was all about himself, how could he receive the Spirit's vision (purpose)? There was no way he was going to fulfil the Spirit's purpose, because he was all about fulfilling his own fleshly purposes!

Are you serving the vision of the Spirit or the vision of the flesh?

"No one lights a lamp and hides it in a jar or puts it under a bed. Instead, he puts it on a stand, so that those who come in can see the light."

Luke 8:16

The light in this parable refers to the Spirit, and the bed to the flesh. What Christ meant is that you cannot hide the Spirit under the flesh. The Spirit is the vision bearer; He sends His vision to your mind, your mind communicates it to your body, and your body acts it out. When the Spirit (vision bearer) is lighted up, the fleshly desires should surrender to the Spirit's vision and die. But if the flesh persists with its own desires, it will suppress the Spirit from communicating His vision to the mind. That is like hiding one's light in a jar or under a bed—the jar or bed being likened to the flesh that is hiding the Spirit's vision.

Therefore, to allow the light (Spirit) to shine forth, the bed (flesh) should be removed from the picture. Notice something else? The lamp is lighted, but what is blocking the light is the bed that is covering it. This refers to people who have received the Spirit but, because they want to fulfill their own selfish desires, they fail to allow the Spirit to communicate His vision (purpose) to them.

The Light of Life

You cannot serve both the Spirit's purposes and the purposes of the flesh; they are in conflict with one another. To fulfill the Spirit's purpose, you need to let go of your own purposes. This is the most difficult test facing born-again Christians, and only a few pass it.

The seed that fell among thorns stands for those who hear, but as they go on their way they are choked by life's worries, riches and pleasures, and they do not mature.
Luke 8:14

The seed here represents those who fail to fulfill the Spirit's vision for them because they are holding onto their own fleshly visions. In their pursuit after riches and pleasures, they have choked the Spirit's vision for their lives. The vision of the flesh has suppressed the vision of the Spirit. The light (Spirit) was put under the bed (flesh); therefore it was prevented from lighting up the house (the person's life).

For there is nothing hidden that will not be disclosed, and nothing concealed that will not be known or brought out into the open.
Luke 8:17

The vision (purpose) of your life is hidden in the Spirit, but it is meant to be disclosed to you. To fulfill this vision from the Spirit, however, you need to bring your fleshly desires under control. Ask yourself: who is in the driver's seat of your life? Is it your flesh (body) or the Spirit? If you allow your body to drive itself, it will kick out the Spirit and bring you to the wrong destination—because your body by itself does not have the true vision (purpose) of your life.

The body is meant to submit itself to the Spirit and to walk in accordance with the Spirit's vision. When this happens, you will be driven by the Spirit's vision and you will reach your rightful destiny. You will find yourself fulfilling your true purpose on earth.

From that time on Jesus began to explain to his disciples that he must go to Jerusalem and suffer many things at the hands of the elders, chief priests and teachers of the law, and that he must be killed and on the third day be raised to life.

Peter took him aside and began to rebuke him. "Never, Lord!" he said. "This shall never happen to you!"

Jesus turned and said to Peter, "Get behind me, Satan! You are a stumbling block to me; you do not have in mind the things of God, but the things of men."

Matthew 16:21-23

The suffering that Christ was talking about here was the pain His body would have to bear when He was tortured and crucified on the cross. It was necessary for Him to submit His body to be beaten and crucified in order to fulfill the vision of the Spirit. It was necessary for Him to overcome the needs of the flesh (to be pain-free) in order for Him to accomplish the purpose for which He came to earth.

Remember that the flesh is often opposing the purposes of the Spirit. The flesh is not willing to face the pain of being tortured and crucified. Therefore, for Christ to accomplish the mission of the Father, He needed to overcome the opposition of the flesh. Christ needed to overcome the opposition of His own body, so that He could be driven by the vision of the Spirit. If Christ had not been able to overcome the opposition of His own flesh, He would not have been able to go through the pain of being tortured and crucified—because His body was not willing to suffer.

It is exactly the same with us: to fulfill the vision of the Spirit, we need to overcome the opposition of the flesh, because often the flesh is not willing to submit to the Spirit. Unless you can overcome the opposition of your flesh, you cannot fulfill the Spirit's purpose for your life.

Then he said to them, "My soul is overwhelmed with sorrow to the point of death. Stay here and keep watch with me."

Going a little farther, he fell with his face to the ground and prayed, "My Father, if it is possible, may this cup be taken from me. Yet not as I will, but as you will."

Matthew 26:38-39

This was the moment when Christ's body was in opposition to the Spirit's vision. It was not the Spirit speaking to Christ at this moment but the flesh. The flesh was looking at the pain it was going to suffer in being tortured and crucified. For Jesus to take the suffering of the cross, He had to overcome the flesh and bring it under submission to the Spirit's will.

So it is with us too; unless we can overcome our body's opposition to the Spirit, we will not be able to fulfill the Spirit's vision for us. Fulfilling the Spirit's vision requires us to deny ourselves (our flesh) so that the Spirit can bring us into alignment with the Father's will.

Then Jesus said to his disciples, "If anyone would come after me, he must deny himself and take up his cross and follow me."

Matthew 16:24

You see, if you want to fulfill the Spirit's vision, you must deny yourself. When Jesus spoke of denying oneself, He was talking about overcoming the body's opposition to the Spirit's vision. Take heed of this:

Denying yourself is not an option but an obligation.

Unless you deny yourself, you cannot follow after the Spirit's vision. The cross you need to take up is that of self-opposition. If you want to follow after Christ, you must take up the cross of overcoming your own flesh. That was what Jesus meant when He said that we must take up our cross and follow Him.

"For whoever wants to save his life will lose it, but whoever loses his life for me will find it."

Matthew 16:25

Here, wanting to save your life means living for your own self-needs (your flesh). You are trying to save your flesh by living according to its demands; but, in so doing, you will lose out on fulfilling the Spirit's vision for your life. When you think you are saving your life by satisfying its demands, you are actually losing your true purpose in life.

Conversely, when you lose yourself by denying the demands of the flesh, you will find the Spirit's vision and walk according to it. Therefore, if you want to find the Spirit's vision, you have to let go of your own vision (the demands of your flesh). You cannot serve both the Spirit's vision and your own self-vision; you will despise the one to please the other.

What good will it be for a man if he gains the whole world, yet forfeits his soul?
Matthew 16:26

What good is it, if we gain everything to satisfy the desires of our flesh, yet forfeit our souls? We forfeit our souls when we live our lives for our own selfish ends and despise the Spirit's vision for our lives.

The Spirit's vision is the true reason for our existence here on earth. If we exist but do nothing to accomplish the Spirit's vision for us, it is as if we never existed at all—because we have not fulfilled our real purpose on earth.

You Cannot Serve Both the Spirit and the Flesh

"Do not store up for yourselves treasures on earth, where moth and rust destroy, and where thieves break in and steal. But store up for yourselves treasures in heaven, where moth and rust do not destroy, and where thieves do not break in and steal."

Matthew 6:19-20

The point Jesus was making was that we should not live life for "self"; we should not allow our lives to be driven by what the flesh considers as "treasures". Why not? Because, when "self" drives your life, the Spirit is unable to drive you to accomplish His purpose for your life. When you live your life to acquire that car, that house, that job, that woman, that man, that business, that position, you miss out on fulfilling the Spirit's vision—because you already have a vision of your own.

You have already set your own target; that is the reason you cannot meet the Spirit's target. While you are in the process of acquiring that car, house, and so on, you are also in the process of missing the mark where the Spirit's vision is concerned. Therefore, living your life to store up treasures for yourself has caused you to fail to fulfill the Spirit's purpose—because you are already satisfying your own self-purpose. Achieving your self-purpose is in direct opposition to accomplishing the Spirit's purpose.

"For where your treasure is, there your heart will be also."

Matthew 6:21

The Light of Life

Your heart is the vision bearer to your body, and your body is driven by the vision that is in your heart. If the vision of your heart is to acquire that house, that car, that business, and so on, your body is going to be driven in accordance with that vision. If self-vision is driving your body, it will kick out the Spirit's vision or relegate it to a back seat in your life.

"The eye is the lamp of the body. If your eyes are good, your whole body will be full of light. But if your eyes are bad, your whole body will be full of darkness."
Matthew 6:22-23

What did Christ mean by saying that the eye is the lamp of the body? He was using our physical eyes as an example of what He wanted us to understand.

Our eyes give us vision. We see where we are going with our eyes; therefore, they are like lamps that light our way. In that sense, our eyes function as the vision bearer for our whole body. But when our eyes are blind, we have no vision and do not know where we are going. Similarly, when we let our self-vision be our eyes, our eyes will be blinded because they do not have the light of the Spirit in them. (Remember *Luke 8:16*?) And so, we will have no vision and will not know where we are going.

When you allow your self-vision to direct your life, you are blocking the Spirit from communicating His vision to you. Your self-vision has blinded you to the Spirit's vision. In other words, that self-vision is preventing you from living your life according to the Spirit's vision—because spiritually you are blind, though you think you can see.

If then the light within you is darkness, how great is that darkness!
Matthew 6:23

The light within you is the Spirit's vision for you. If that vision is blocked by your self-vision, how great is your darkness regarding your purpose in life! How can you know the true purpose of your existence, if you are blinding yourself to the Spirit's vision because of your own self-vision?

"No one can serve two masters. Either he will hate the one and love the other, or he will be devoted to the one and despise the other. You cannot serve both God and Money."
Matthew 6:24

The point is this: you cannot be driven by two conflicting purposes (making money and obeying the will of God) at the same time. You cannot live a self-serving life if you want to serve God. It is either self-will or God's will that is directing your life; you cannot have both in the driver's seat.

CHAPTER 6

You Are Forgiven!

How man turned from serving God to serving his own needs

God banished Adam and Eve from the Garden of Eden after the fall. Thereafter, man's needs were no longer God's responsibility, and man became responsible for his own needs.

When man was still in the Garden of Eden, he was serving God's purposes, and all his needs were God's responsibility. However, when the devil deceived him into disobeying God (by eating fruit from the tree of the knowledge of good and evil), man was no longer serving the purposes of God but the purposes of his deceiver, the devil.

So the LORD God banished him from the Garden of Eden to work the ground from which he had been taken. After he drove the man out, he placed on the east side of the Garden of Eden cherubim and a flaming sword flashing back and forth to guard the way to the tree of life.

Genesis 3:23-24

After the fall, man no longer served the Kingdom of God, which he was created to serve. He began serving another kingdom—the kingdom of darkness (the kingdom of the devil). Remember that, while he was in the Kingdom of God, man had all his needs met by God. But, now that he was in the kingdom of darkness, man must supply his own needs by the sweat of his brow. Man began to experience all kinds of suffering because he was out of the Kingdom of God, where all his needs had been provided for. All this suffering came about as a result of disobeying God's command.

To Adam he said, "Because you listened to your wife and ate from the tree about which I commanded you, 'You must not eat of it,'

"Cursed is the ground because of you; through painful toil you will eat of it all the days of your life. It will produce thorns and thistles for you, and you will eat the plants of the field. By the sweat of your brow you will eat your food..."

Genesis 3:17-19

This can be likened to someone who breaks the law and is sentenced by the Magistrate to serve time in prison. So, when he is in prison, his way of life changes. He no longer has access to the possessions, resources and people he had before he was jailed. All the suffering he undergoes in prison is the result of his violating the law. So it is the same with us: all the suffering we undergo in this world is the result of the sin of one man, Adam.

Here is another illustration: suppose you worked as the manager of a company that provided you with a house, a car, medical benefits, and everything else you needed. Then it happened that you violated one of the company's policies and, as a result, the company decided to fire you. So, now that you are fired, you begin to suffer. You no longer have an income or the benefits that came with the job. You no longer have a house or car; you are without food or medical benefits; in short, you have lost everything as a result of violating the company's rules.

So, to keep from starving, this is what you do:

- ❖ You toil under the hot sun to make a living;
- ❖ You cheat people to make a living;
- ❖ You steal people's things to make a living;
- ❖ You prostitute yourself to make a living;
- ❖ You sell drugs to make a living;
- ❖ You rob banks to make a living;
- ❖ You kill people to make a living.

But now the company you worked for has realized that you are suffering as a result of losing your job. And they have sent a delegate to deliver this message to you: "YOU ARE FORGIVEN!"

What do these words tell you? This should be the greatest news for you: it means you can get your job back! It means all that you have lost will be restored to you when you are reinstated in your position:

- ❖ Your income will be restored to you;
- ❖ Your house will be restored to you;
- ❖ Your car will be restored to you;
- ❖ Your medical benefits will be restored to you.

In short, when you are restored to your position, everything you lost will be restored to you. Do you understand that? This means you can stop cheating people, stealing from them, prostituting yourself, selling drugs, robbing banks, and killing people to make a living. You had to do all this to make a living because you had lost your position. But now the good news is that the company has given you back your position. All you lacked, you only lacked because you had lost your position. But, since you have been restored to your original position, everything that had been taken away has now been returned to you.

So it is with us: when, through Adam, we lost our positions in the Kingdom of God, we lost all the benefits that came with those positions. But now, through Jesus' sacrifice on the cross, we have been forgiven and restored to our kingdom positions.

For just as through the disobedience of the one man the many were made sinners, so also through the obedience of the one man the many will be made righteous.

Romans 5:19

Now man can turn from serving his own needs to serving God

When God reinstated you and me in His Kingdom, He gave us back all that we lost when we lost our kingdom positions. This means that everything we lost has been restored to us.

- ❖ You don't need money but your position;
- ❖ You don't need a house but your position;
- ❖ You don't need a car but your position;
- ❖ You don't need medical aid but your position.

All the problems that came to you were the result of your losing your position. But when you regained your position, you also regained everything you had lost. Therefore, you should stop seeking after things and begin to seek after your kingdom position. You should stop serving your own needs and begin to serve God.

But seek first his kingdom and his righteousness, and all these things will be given to you as well.

Matthew 6:33

Chapter 7

Saved in the Name of Jesus Christ

When Adam sinned in the Garden of Eden, he sold himself (and through him all mankind) to the kingdom of darkness. Man was taken hostage by the devil, and he needed a saviour to save him. So God sent His Son Jesus Christ to save man from the kingdom of darkness.

Remember that, before Adam sinned, man was made in the image and likeness of God and of His son Jesus Christ. Before the fall, man was functioning in the exact same way in which God and His son Jesus functioned. All the functions of God and His son Jesus were within human beings, because we were in God's class. But when the devil deceived man and caused him to sin by eating the forbidden fruit, the likeness of God within man was degraded. Because of this, man needed a saviour to redeem him and restore him back to the likeness of God and His son Jesus Christ.

Suppose you purchased a TV set from a certain store, and you got a one-year guarantee for that TV. And suppose, before the end of the guarantee period, you realized that the TV was no longer functioning as it should. What do you do then? You take it back to the store where you bought it from, and that store will replace it with a perfectly-functioning TV of exactly the same model and brand. This means the replacement set will have all the features of the previous TV, because the store has to give you a TV of the same model and brand.

What I want you to see is that the store should replace your TV with another set that functions perfectly and is exactly the same model and brand as the one you purchased. The replacement set should be identical to the one that was damaged. If the store were to give you a model or brand of TV that is different from the one you purchased, it means the store has robbed you—or you have robbed the store.

Now, you and I were created in the likeness of God and His son Jesus Christ. But, because Adam sinned, man stopped functioning the way God had planned that he should. So man needs a redeemer to restore him to his original functionality—and the only two redeemers who can do so are God and His Son Jesus Christ, because these are the only two beings who are in man's class.

Do you understand what I am trying to tell you here? Just as that specific TV can only be redeemed by a TV of the same model and brand, so it is with man's redemption. The only persons who can redeem him are the ones who are in his class. In other words, the only persons to redeem mankind are the ones who are identical to man's previous condition of perfection.

All the problems that you encountered in your previous defective TV are resolved with the replacement model. Can you see that? Christ Jesus came to earth as a replacement model to resolve all the problems of defective man. He came to bring us back to our previous condition of perfection before the fall. This means:

- His healthy eyes replaced my sick eyes;
- His healthy ears replaced my sick ears;
- His healthy head replaced my sick head;
- His healthy heart replaced my sick heart;
- His healthy lungs replaced my sick lungs;
- His healthy arms replaced my sick arms;
- His healthy hands replaced my sick hands;
- His healthy stomach replaced my sick stomach;
- His healthy legs replaced my sick legs;
- His whole righteous body replaced my whole sinful body.

What does it mean to be saved in the name of Jesus Christ?

This means you are no longer doing things in your own name, but in the name of the One who saved you—Jesus Christ—since He died for you. You are now living in His name and not in your own name anymore; this is because your name was debased through Adam's fall.

For we know that our old self was crucified with him so that the body of sin might be done away with, that we should no longer be slaves to sin—because anyone who has died has been freed from sin.

Now if we died with Christ, we believe that we will also live with him.

Romans 6:6-8

When you accepted Jesus as your Lord and Saviour, you died to your sinful self, and you now live in the righteousness of Christ Jesus. You are no longer living in your own name, but in the name of Jesus Christ, because He died for you on the cross. Christ did not die for Himself, but He died for you and me. In other words, when Christ died, you also died with Him. This is the reason we say, "In the name of Jesus, you are saved." It is because you have escaped from living in the name of Adam (the fallen man) and are now living in the name of Jesus (the righteous Man).

You were once living in the name of Adam, the first man from whom we are all descended. But since Jesus died in the name of Adam, it is as if Adam died through Christ's crucifixion. So Adam no longer exists in you, but Christ does. Therefore, you are saved in the name of Jesus. But this is only applicable to those who have accepted Jesus as their Lord and Saviour, not to those who do not believe in Him.

This means that all of Adam's (man's) sicknesses, diseases, suffering, poverty and pain were taken by Jesus, because Jesus died in the name of Adam (and therefore, in your name). And all of Jesus' health, power, wisdom and wealth are now yours in the name of Jesus. You are saved in the name of Jesus, because the name of Jesus (which you have inherited) brought you salvation and everything that was His—health, wealth, wisdom and power.

Let me explain it this way: suppose you were sentenced to life imprisonment for a crime you had committed. And you had a rich brother who owned a big house, five luxury cars, and 100 thousand billion dollars. Now suppose your brother in compassion approached the judge and offered to serve the life sentence in your stead, while you live his life.

What does that mean to you? It means that the punishment for your sins has all been laid upon your brother, while his riches—his house, cars and vast sums of money—have all been given to you. Do you really understand that? This means you are living your life in your brother's name, and your brother is living his life in your name. This means you are saved from all the sufferings of life imprisonment. I pray that you get the full meaning of this revelation.

So it is with all who have accepted Jesus as their Saviour. We are saved in the name of Jesus. We have inherited all His wealth, and all our sins have been laid upon Him.

For Christ's love compels us, because we are convinced that one died for all, and therefore all died. And he died for all, that those who live should no longer live for themselves but for him who died for them and was raised again.
2 Corinthians 5:14-15

The day you received Jesus Christ into your life, you died to your own life and began to live for the One (Christ) who died for you. But, since you have been used to living according to the way of the fallen man (Adam), you have to fight to change your old mindset. It is a battle of the mind, because your mind is used to Adam's way of life. But now Adam's lifestyle must die in you, because you are no longer living in Adam's name, but in the name of Jesus. You must conform to Christ's lifestyle and bury Adam's lifestyle, because Adam (the sinful man) is dead and Christ (the righteous man) now lives in you.

Most Christians have disappointed God because they are satisfied with just going to church. They miss the big picture regarding their salvation, which is to experience the complete power of Jesus in their lives. In other words, the purpose of salvation extends…

- Far beyond church attendance;
- Far beyond getting a job;
- Far beyond getting married.

Since we are now living in Jesus' name, God expects you and me to do all that Christ had been doing on earth—such as healing the sick, opening the eyes of the blind, and raising the dead to life.

- It is not enough to say, "I am saved."
- It is not enough to say, "I am born again."
- It is not enough to say, "I go to church."
- It is not enough to say, "I am a worship leader."
- It is not enough to say, "I am a pastor."
- It is not enough to say, "I am an evangelist."

Why is it not enough? Because the purpose of salvation is to experience the *full* power of Christ Jesus manifested in our lives.

Chapter 8

Every Promise Is Governed by Certain Principles

The world teaches us that success can be found somewhere out there. People often abandon their homelands to search for success in other countries. But consider this truth: all that makes any product function successfully has already been built into the product itself. Every purpose that the manufacturer has intended the product to fulfil is found within the product itself. The product does not have to search for its success elsewhere; its success lies within itself.

Is this not true of God's product (man) too? Your success is not found somewhere in the world but within yourself. You miss it when you try to find it in the world, because God has placed within you everything He planned for you to fulfil on earth.

Your body is a package of everything you need for success, for within yourself are treasures this world knows nothing about. Most people think their bodies are made only for eating, drinking and dressing up.

Every Promise Is Governed by Certain Principles

But look at what God says:

"Consider how the lilies grow. They do not labour or spin. Yet I tell you, not even Solomon in all his splendour was dressed like one of these. If that is how God clothes the grass of the field, which is here today, and tomorrow is thrown into the fire, how much more will he clothe you, O you of little faith!"

Luke 12:27-28

Think for a moment about those lilies. Have you noticed how beautiful a lily looks? The question is, where does that beauty come from? Does a lily work to make itself look so beautiful? The answer is No!

Lilies never work. The truth is, all the beauty that we see on the outside of a lily does not come from somewhere else but from within the flower itself. Every lily's beauty is contained within itself: its petals have their origin inside the flower, where they are produced; and its colours likewise have their origin inside the flower, where they are produced.

Does the flower work to make itself beautiful? We know it doesn't labour or spin, but all its beauty is already there within itself. As the lily grows, enduring rain and all other kinds of weather that come against it, it begins to produce its beauty from within itself. In other words, there are internal stores of beauty that are manifested externally. Do you understand that?

The lily's beauty was already designed when God made it, so that as it grows it takes on its beautiful shape. It doesn't go somewhere else to look for its beauty, but beauty lies within itself. Likewise its destiny; a lily's destiny lies within itself. For it to find its destiny, it doesn't need to look elsewhere but only within itself. Its treasure is hidden within itself and not anywhere else. Its destiny is already complete; the lily just has to wait for it to arrive. As the flower grows, it doesn't need to search for its destiny—No! Its destiny has already been designed by its Maker. It will only delay or derail its destiny if it insists on following another destiny that is not its own.

Similarly, man's destiny is already complete; what we should be has already been designed by our Maker. But we delay or derail our destiny when we follow a destiny that is not ours. God has already prepared your destiny for you; He is just waiting for you to arrive. The reality is that everyone's destiny is complete; it is up to us to find our destiny.

We should stop looking elsewhere, because our destiny is within ourselves. As the flower's destiny is within itself, so is man's destiny. This is the reason Jesus said that we should look at the flowers of the field—just so that we will learn that our destiny is not somewhere else, but only within ourselves.

Listen: your destiny is not somewhere else, but is within yourself. You will be delayed in finding it, or even miss it, if you insist on looking for it elsewhere.

EVERY PROMISE IS GOVERNED BY CERTAIN PRINCIPLES

Whatever exists has already been named, and what man is has been known; no man can contend with one who is stronger than he.

Ecclesiastes 6:10

The point that King Solomon was trying to make in the scripture passage above was that, before we were born, the purpose for which we were on earth had already been destined—even before we knew about it. In other words, each one of us just unfolds into the shape that God has already designed us to be.

Everyone's purpose on earth is already known to God because He designed us. What makes us miss our destiny is striving to become what we are not. It is very possible to miss God's plan for us if we insist on holding onto our own plans. Actually, most people die without accomplishing God's plan for their lives because they insist on following their own plans.

Who you are is already known to God; but you delay or even miss it and waste God's time when you do what you are not meant to do. Your destiny was decided for you even before you were born. It is your responsibility to unlock it—it is all up to you.

The word of the LORD came to me, saying,
   "Before I formed you in the womb I knew you,
     before you were born I set you apart;
   I appointed you as a prophet to the nations."

Jeremiah 1:4-5

The Light of Life

Do you notice the sequence of events here? Jeremiah was appointed to be a prophet *before* he was formed in his mother's womb, not after.

As is written in the book of the words of Isaiah the prophet:
"A voice of one calling in the desert,
'Prepare the way for the Lord,
make straight paths for him.
Every valley shall be filled in,
every mountain and hill made low.
The crooked roads should become straight,
the rough ways smooth.
And all mankind will see God's salvation.'"

Luke 3:4-6

The truth is that there is always a method you need to follow to achieve anything. If you don't follow the correct method, you won't attain your goal. You need to follow the principles in order to gain whatever has been promised to you; and, if you don't follow those principles, you won't receive the promised reward.

For example, if you wake up in the morning and you don't wash yourself, and you do the same the next day, and you don't wash yourself for the whole week—what do you think will happen to you? People will tell you, "Brother (or sister), you stink."

Now the question is, why do you stink? The answer is simple: because you haven't washed. You stink because you ignored the principle of bathing.

EVERY PROMISE IS GOVERNED BY CERTAIN PRINCIPLES

This means you need to obey the principle of bathing in order to be clean. The principle of bathing can never be replaced by any other principle.

You can put on your best suit but, if you haven't bathed, you will still stink. Wearing a suit doesn't take away dirt. You can wear a beautiful dress but, if you haven't bathed, you will still stink—because the principle of bathing cannot be replaced by your nice dress. Only bathing can take away dirt from your body. This means the principle of bathing is irreplaceable.

Again, if you are hungry, the only way to get rid of those hunger pangs is to eat food. You can bathe and dress beautifully, but you will still be hungry. Everyone may praise you for the beautiful clothes you are wearing, but that doesn't take away your hunger. The only way to overcome hunger is to eat food.

I hope you perceive what I am showing you here: that there are specific principles you need to apply for every promise made to you. This means that there is a certain principle to apply for every promise; and that principle can never be replaced by another principle. If you don't apply the principle, you will not be able to see the promised result of that principle.

- ❖ If you don't bathe, you won't be clean;
- ❖ If you don't eat, you won't be filled.

God's Word (the Bible) contains many promises. But most people do not eat of those promises, and they are not filled — simply because they do not apply the principles in the Word of God. If we do not act on the Word of God, we will never receive the fulfilment of the promises which are in His Word.

When we begin to act on the Word of God in our lives, we bring forth the promises which are in the Word of God. Most people pray, "God, please do something about this situation," but what they don't understand is that God (Jesus Christ) has already done everything about their situation on the cross of Calvary. God is waiting for them to apply the principle that will bring forth what they are asking for. Most people don't know that God has already healed them. They don't know that God has already provided for all their needs. All they need to do is to apply the right principle in God's Word that will bring forth their healing and meet their needs.

For example: if a husband and wife want to have a baby, they will have to apply the principle that will bring forth a baby. What is that principle? They will have to have sex together, because sex is the principle to bring forth their baby. If they want a baby but they do not apply the principle, how can they expect to have a baby? They cannot blame God for not having a baby, but only themselves. Why? Because they are not applying the principle that will bring forth their baby. Think about it.

God has already given them a baby, but they need to apply the principle (sex) that will bring forth their baby. If they don't have sex, they won't have a baby. Not because God does not want to give them a baby—No! But because they are not applying the principle that will bring forth their baby. Isn't that true?

So it is with everything else that we are asking for. God has already provided for all our needs, but it is up to us to apply the principles in His Word that will bring forth the promised provision. If you do not apply the Word of God in your life, you will not eat of the promises in it. Therefore you cannot blame God for not receiving what you need, but only yourself. You have everything within you; but, until you apply the principles that will bring you what you need, you will remain in need.

Apply the Word of God to your life

The Word of God is the key to your prosperity; it is like rain falling on the earth and making it flourish. This means there are already plants inside the ground waiting to emerge, but it all depends on the rain. So, inside you there is already prosperity waiting to come out, but it will only come out when the Word of God is applied by you—then prosperity will come out.

"As the rain and the snow come down from heaven, and do not return to it without watering the earth and making it bud and flourish, so that it yields seed for the sower and bread for the eater, so is my word that goes out from my mouth: It will not return to me empty, but will accomplish what I desire and achieve the purpose for which I sent it."

Isaiah 55:10-11

Most people die in poverty because they don't apply God's Word to their lives. Therefore, they fail to bring forth the prosperity planted within them. They might know how to read the Word and even speak about it; but most people fail to apply it. Therefore, they don't eat the fruit of it—because it is not just reading the Word that brings prosperity, not just talking the Word, but it is implementing the Word.

It is like a sick man who goes to see the doctor, and the doctor gives him the right medicine. But, when this man gets home, he decides not to take the medicine. So he dies. Whose fault is it then? The doctor's or the patient's? Certainly it is the patient's fault! Why? Because the doctor gave the medicine to the patient, but the patient chose not to use it.

This is exactly what happens to most of God's children—they die in their poverty, even though God gave them His Word to make them prosper. They choose not to use it. So they die because they don't use the information (the Word of God) given to them.

Your actions speak louder than your words

Praying is not just talking; true prayer is making a decision and acting on it. Most of us do not receive what we ask from God because we are still trusting in our own plans more than we trust in God. You can talk to God but, if your actions contradict your words, you will receive nothing from Him. Talking is necessary, but action is more necessary than talking.

"What do you think? There was a man who had two sons. He went to the first and said, 'Son, go and work today in the vineyard.'

"'I will not,' he answered, but later he changed his mind and went.

"Then the father went to the other son and said the same thing. He answered, 'I will, sir,' but he did not go.

"Which of the two did what his father wanted?"

"The first," they answered.

Matthew 21:28-31

Can you see now that what you *do* is more important than what you say? The first son told his father he was not going to obey him but later, without even telling his father, he changed his mind and went to work. And his father loved what he *did*—not what he said at the beginning. His father loved his actions, not his words. The second son told his father that he would go and work, but he never went. The father wasn't happy with him, because he didn't put his words into action. So, what you *do* is more important than what you say. You can pray to God, but if you don't act on His Word, you will receive nothing from Him. Talking is not enough, but doing is.

We are servants of the Word and the Word serves us in return

One day the disciples asked Jesus to increase their faith. This turned into a very interesting conversation between Jesus and His disciples. Let us examine it:

The apostles said to the Lord, "Increase our faith!"

He replied, "If you have faith as small as a mustard seed, you can say to this mulberry tree, 'Be uprooted and planted in the sea,' and it will obey you.

"Suppose one of you had a servant ploughing or looking after the sheep. Would he say to the servant when he comes in from the field, 'Come along now and sit down to eat'? Would he not rather say, 'Prepare my supper, get yourself ready and wait on me while I eat and drink; after that you may eat and drink'?

"Would he thank the servant because he did what he was told to do? So you also, when you have done everything you were told to do, should say, 'We are unworthy servants; we have only done our duty.'"

Luke 17:5-10

I want us to examine Jesus' words carefully here. He was replying to His disciples' request, "Increase our faith." He answered them by giving the example of the servant and his master. What was the point that Jesus wanted to make here? It was this: *you will never get paid until you do your duty.* You do your duty first, and then your master pays you.

What Jesus was saying, in the context of His disciples' request, was this: you have to be a servant of the Word first before the Word serves you in return. If I were asked to describe what faith is, I would say it is *doing* what the Word says—not just talking about it, but putting it into action. If you look at Jesus' parable, you will see that the servant *did* what his master asked him to do, and the master gave him what he promised. The servant served the master first, and then the master served him in return.

Jesus was showing His disciples what faith is all about—acting on what the Word says. Our actions prove that we truly believe in the Word of God and, after we serve our faith, then our faith will serve us in return. How do we serve our faith? We act on what the Word says.

When was Abraham considered to be a blessed, righteous man and a friend of God? It was *after* he acted on what the word of God told him to do. In other words, he served his faith by his actions, and thereafter—because of his actions—his faith served him in return. He was acknowledged as a friend of God, a righteous man, and someone greatly blessed.

The Light of Life

These were all credited to him *after* he acted on what he was told. And everyone who puts God's Word into action will receive what Abraham received.

So, remember this: going to church, being a church member, or quoting the Bible are not of primary importance. It is *acting* on God's Word that makes you righteous, blessed and a friend of God.

You foolish man, do you want evidence that faith without deeds is useless? Was not our ancestor Abraham considered righteous for what he did when he offered his son Isaac on the altar? You see that his faith and actions were working together, and his faith was made complete by what he did. And the scripture was fulfilled that says, "Abraham believed God, and it was credited to him as righteousness," and he was called God's friend. You see that a person is justified by what he does and not by faith alone.

James 2:20-24

For example: when you are driving a car, what do you do? You serve it first, and afterwards it serves you in return. You press the clutch and change the gear—then the car moves. If you don't do that, the car will not serve you in return—not because the car is defective but because you are not doing what needs to be done to the car. The car will never move until you do what you must do to it. Think about that.

You serve your car before it serves you. If you don't serve your car by pressing on its accelerator, its speed will never increase. You have got to serve it first by pressing on the accelerator, and then the car will accelerate. At night, you serve your car by switching on its lights—then they will serve you and enable you to see the road. Do you understand? People who don't know how to drive don't do what the car requires them to do, and therefore they don't get the benefit of its service. But everyone who does what the car requires him to do receives its service in return. There is no partiality—you only have to do what is required of you, and you will be paid in return.

It is exactly the same with God—He does not show partiality. We only have to do what He requires of us, and we will enjoy the fruit of our actions. Those who don't eat the fruit are those who don't do what the Word of God requires them to do. If we act on the Word, the Word will serve us in return. Remember, it is not quoting the Word or talking about the Word that brings its fruit back to you, but it is acting on the Word that will bear fruit.

After Jesus taught His disciples this truth, He also proved it to them:

Now on his way to Jerusalem, Jesus travelled along the border between Samaria and Galilee. As he was going into a village, ten men who had leprosy met him. They stood at a distance and called out in a loud voice, "Jesus, Master, have pity on us!"

When he saw them, he said, "Go, show yourselves to the priests." And as they went, they were cleansed.

Luke 17:11-14

Consider this: firstly, these men weren't even close to Jesus, they were at a distance. Secondly, they considered Jesus as their Master, and they saw themselves as His servants. This was the reason they said, "Jesus, *Master*, have pity on us!" Remember that this happened after Jesus had told His disciples the parable of the servant and his master; now Jesus was about to prove the truth of the parable.

When the ten men said, "Jesus, Master, have pity on us!" He responded by saying, "Go, show yourselves to the priests." Consider this: Jesus' words didn't bring them their healing, but what brought about their healing was their acting on His word. As they were going to show themselves to the priests—just as Jesus had commanded—on their way, they realized, 'Oh! We are cleansed of our leprosy!'

The ten men acted on the word of the Master, and their action brought about their healing—it was as simple as that. This incident proved to the disciples that they should be servants of the Word before the Word would serve them in return. We too should be servants of our faith; then our faith will serve us. What happened to those ten men can also happen to anyone who will put the Word of God into action. Be a servant of the Word, and the Word of God will serve you in return—that is called faith. It is important to act on the Word; then the Word will act in your situation.

CHAPTER 9

The Secret of Our Battle

Putting off the old self (Adam) and Putting on the new self (Christ)

"No one after drinking old wine wants the new, for he says, 'The old is better.'"

Luke 5:39

Do you perceive the wisdom of Jesus' words here? He knows that, when our minds are used to a certain way of doing things, it becomes very difficult for us to accept a new way, even though the new way of doing things is better.

There was a time when I used a certain phone for two years, and I loved it dearly. But one day I lost it and got another one—different and better, compared to my previous phone. I thought my new phone worked the same way as my old one but, when I tried to use it in the same way, I realized the new phone didn't use the same system as the old one. It took time for me to get used to the functions of this new phone; I wasn't familiar with its system, and this made me think the old phone's system was better. I believe most of you will be able to relate to this.

The key to discovering the benefits of our new life in Christ is to forget about Adam's old system and look forward to Christ's new system of living. But when we start to do this, it becomes painfully clear to us that there is a battle raging in our minds.

Most Christians blame the devil for every bad thing that happens in their lives, because they don't understand that the power of evil was defeated on the cross of Calvary. However, there is still a battle to be fought in our minds. You hear Christians saying things like, "The devil told me to do it," not knowing that it was not the devil who was speaking to them, but their old nature.

When you have grown a bit in Christ, you begin to realize that you are fighting against yourself— against the old system of the old man, Adam. So the battle is not between you and the devil, as most people think; fighting the devil was never your responsibility, but God's. And He has already won that battle, through the crucifixion of Christ on the cross. So your battle is now between the new creation (Christ) and the old nature (Adam). In other words, you are battling in your mind to accept Christ's new system and to let go of Adam's old system.

Remember that the life of Adam is the life that most of us live in this present age—we live to save ourselves, not knowing that God has already saved us. Living for our needs is the life we began to live when God banished us from His kingdom. But since God has brought us back to His kingdom through Christ, we no longer live to supply our needs; instead, we now live to do God's will, while God supplies our needs. However, the problem is that man is so used to the old system of living for his own needs that he cannot pay attention to what God is telling him.

You were taught, with regard to your former way of life, to put off your old self, which is being corrupted by its deceitful desires; to be made new in the attitude of your minds; and to put on the new self, created to be like God in true righteousness and holiness.

Ephesians 4:22-24

People think that their old system of living for their needs is better than the new system of living for God, simply because they are used to the old system. But this is not true; it is much better to live to do God's will and to have our needs supplied through God's abundant provision for us.

Until you get a taste of the new drink, you will always think that what you are drinking now is better. This is exactly what Christ said: until you test the new system, the old system will always seem to you to be better—not because it really is better, but because you are used to it.

We are dead to the realm of Adam but alive to the realm of Christ

We don't fight as this world fights, and we are not living our lives as this world lives—because we have died to this world but are alive in Christ's realm. Do you get this? We have died to this world, and we are now living our lives in another world—the world of Jesus. That is why we get healed of the world's sicknesses; it is a sign that we are not of this world. This world's sicknesses cannot harm us, because we are in another world, the world of Jesus.

God saved us from this world and placed us in Christ's world. This is the reason why, when we believe in the name of Jesus, we get healed of the sicknesses that afflict people in this present world. This is evidence that we are not of this present world, but belong to the realm of Christ. We are dead to the present world of Adam (even though we live in it), but alive in the heavenly realm of Christ. This is because we no longer live in the name of Adam but in the name of Jesus Christ, who died for us. We are saved from Adam's name into Christ's name.

Consider this: when a person is dead, you don't educate him about the laws of this world because he can't break them anymore. Why? Because he is dead to the world, even though we can still touch his body. The fact is, *he is dead to this world.*

You cannot tell a dead body the following:

- ❖ Don't steal;
- ❖ Don't drink and drive;
- ❖ Don't murder.

You cannot tell a dead man to obey these laws—because he is no longer alive, but dead. It is obvious that, because he is dead, he will never steal or murder anymore. All the laws of this world no longer apply to him; he is dead to them. Do you see this?

So it is the same with us: we are dead to Adam's world but alive in Christ's realm. We are governed by the new laws in Christ's realm. The laws of Adam's world govern those who are still living in that world, not those who are dead to it. The sicknesses of Adam's world are the sicknesses of those who are still living in it, not those who are dead to it. I hope you understand this.

> *Or don't you know that all of us who were baptized into Christ Jesus were baptized into his death? We were therefore buried with him through baptism into death in order that, just as Christ was raised from the dead through the glory of the Father,* ***we too may live a new life.***
>
> Romans 6:3-4

Take the example of a woman who is married to an abusive husband. When her husband dies and she marries another man, she is freed from all the beatings she suffered at the hands of her first husband. Similarly, now that we are dead to Adam's realm and married into Jesus' realm, we are freed from the sufferings we endured when we were still living in Adam's realm. Now we live in a new realm—the realm of Christ Jesus.

So all the problems you encountered when you were living in Adam's realm are to be left there; they no longer exist in this new realm of Christ. In other words, those were the problems of the past, not of the present realm. But, even though you are now in Christ's realm, you can still find yourself living like you used to in Adam's realm—if you do not reprogram your mind. So it is with most Christians: although they claim to be born again, their minds are still not reprogrammed for their new life. And this makes them miss the benefits of life in Christ Jesus.

Forgetting the past (Adam) and focusing on the future (Christ)

Not that I have already obtained all this, or have already been made perfect, but I press on to take hold of that for which Christ Jesus took hold of me. Brothers, I do not consider myself yet to have taken hold of it. But one thing I do: Forgetting what is behind and straining toward what is ahead...

Philippians 3:12-13

This means we are to forget about the principles of Adam's world. When we enter into Christ's realm, we must forget all the principles which governed us in man's world. For example, in man's world the key to success is education; but, in Christ's world, the key to success is obedience to God's Word. I am not against education but, according to the standard God uses to measure success, having a certain qualification doesn't mean you are successful. Success is not defined by your teacher, mother, or anyone else; but true success is only defined by God.

God is the One who created you, and He knows the work for which He put you here on earth. You can have good qualifications and a wonderful job but, if you are not doing what you have been sent to do, you are not successful—because the plan for your life is not with you, but with Him. So your success can never be measured by education or by how many qualifications you have—No, not at all!

The apostle Paul was one of the few people who understood that, by receiving Jesus into his life, he was living in Christ's realm. All his needs would be supplied from Christ's realm. We hear him saying, "I have no confidence in the flesh." (*Philippians 3*) What did he mean by this? Paul was trying to tell us that he was no longer dependent on the qualifications he acquired in this world, but totally on Christ's realm.

THE LIGHT OF LIFE

But our citizenship is in heaven. And we eagerly await a Saviour from there, the Lord Jesus Christ.

Philippians 3:20

Paul knew that he was dead to this world but alive to Christ's world in heaven. He no longer lived his life according to the principles of this world but the principles of Christ's world. As Christians, we have a new citizenship in heaven through Christ. We are governed by heavenly principles because we have a heavenly citizenship through Jesus. This is why God gave us the Bible, which is the constitution governing those who are in Christ's realm.

We are different from the people of the world; their success is measured by accomplishing the things of this world, whereas our success is measured by accomplishing the things of God. However, most Christians still follow the laws of Adam's world, although they are in Christ's world. So they fail to receive the treasures in Christ's realm, because those treasures are released to you only when you apply the law that governs this realm—that is, the Word of God.

What most Christians fail to understand is that we are now living our lives in the name of Jesus. And what belongs to Jesus Christ (heaven) also belongs to us. But until we lose the system of man's world, we will never gain the things of Christ's world (heaven).

Losing the world to gain heaven

I press on toward the goal to win the prize for which God has called me heavenward in Christ Jesus.
Philippians 3:14

What is the prize of our salvation? It is the heavenly treasure that is contained in Christ Jesus. Heaven was inside Christ, and He displayed it to us through all He did when He was in the world. Through the heavenly power that was contained within Him:

- He healed the sick;
- He made the cripple walk;
- He made the blind see;
- He made the deaf hear;
- He made the dumb speak;
- He changed water into wine;
- He provided food for the people;
- He is the solution to all the world's problems.

Now, since Christ's name is given to us, that heavenly treasure is now inherited by us, and we should display it to the world. This is God's expectation for the Church. This is the ultimate goal of our salvation. Because we have taken the name of Jesus, we are living in His name in order to do what He did.

The Light of Life

But whatever was to my profit I now consider loss for the sake of Christ. What is more, I consider everything a loss compared to the surpassing greatness of knowing Christ Jesus my Lord, for whose sake I have lost all things. I consider them rubbish, that I may gain Christ and be found in him, not having a righteousness of my own that comes from the law, but that which is through faith in Christ...
Philippians 3:7-9

Paul lost all his own benefits to gain what belonged to his new name (Christ). Most Christians do not truly understand what it means to be in Christ, so they miss the benefits that are in Christ's name— because they feel they cannot afford to lose their own benefits.

Paul discovered that the secret of entering Christ's world was to lose the things of his own world. To the extent that he relied on the things he had accomplished through the flesh, he could not gain the things of Christ. So he said, "The secret is to throw away all the things from myself so that I can gain all the things that belong to my new realm in Christ."

You cannot pour tea into a cup that is full of juice; you have to throw the juice out so that you can have space to pour the tea. If you cannot sacrifice the juice by throwing it out, you cannot have tea in the cup. So, in order to gain the wealth of Christ's realm, you have to sacrifice the wealth of Adam's world. Until you sacrifice the wealth of Adam's world, you cannot gain the wealth of Christ's realm.

Chapter 10

The Keys to Your Destiny

There is a purpose behind everything that happens in your life

We see this in Joseph's life; there was a season when it was necessary for him to be hated by his brothers: "[T]hey hated him and could not speak a kind word to him." (*Genesis 37:4*). Why? Because if they had loved him, they wouldn't have sold him to the Ishmaelites, who sold him to Pharaoh. The season of hatred served an important purpose, which was to take Joseph to Egypt. Hatred made his brothers sell Joseph to the Midianites, who delivered him to his destiny in Egypt. In addition, when he was in Egypt, Pharaoh's wife accused Joseph of rape. The rape accusation led him to prison—right where God wanted him to be, in order to fulfil his destiny.

Consider this: everything that happened in Joseph's life didn't happen to put him down, but it was part of God's plan to lead him to his destiny. Each daily trouble was there to achieve the purpose for which Joseph had been destined. Now we see the fulfilment of Jesus' words: "Each day has enough trouble of its own." (*Matthew 6:34*)

The Light of Life

Upon his release from prison, Joseph was put in charge of the whole land of Egypt:

So Pharaoh said to Joseph, "I hereby put you in charge of the whole land of Egypt." Then Pharaoh took his signet ring from his finger and put it on Joseph's finger. He dressed him in robes of fine linen and put a gold chain around his neck. He had him ride in a chariot as his second-in-command, and men shouted before him, "Make way!"

Genesis 41:41-43

God's plan for Joseph was accomplished, but think of what he went through to reach his destiny. Each trouble Joseph faced was part of God's plan to bring him to his destiny.

If you are a child of God, you need to understand this: nothing happens in your life to destroy you, but everything happens to bring you to your destiny. When you understand this, you will be able to rejoice in whatever situation you find yourself—because you know that your Father God is working towards something great for you in the end.

Nothing seems to be any good while it is under construction—think about the house you lived in before it was completed. It looked ugly and totally undesirable, full of stones and rubble. But now you like it! It is the same with the road to your destiny—it might feel painful, distressing and discouraging now, but in the end you will arrive at your destiny.

Most people are so programmed to focus on tomorrow that they don't live in the here and now

"Therefore do not worry about tomorrow, for tomorrow will worry about itself. Each day has enough trouble of its own."

Matthew 6:34

How can I *not* worry about tomorrow? I know from my own experience that it is very difficult not to worry about tomorrow. Most people are so worried about tomorrow that they never enjoy today. Then, when tomorrow arrives, they don't enjoy it either, because they are still worried about the next tomorrow. So they never really live their lives—because they are always living for a tomorrow that never comes.

Many people are always asking questions about tomorrow, so much so that they lose focus on the here and now. They fail to live life today because they are trying to live tomorrow's life today. This means most people die without truly living life at all.

God wants us to live for today. That is why He said, "Do not worry about tomorrow"—because people who are worried about tomorrow never live life in the here and now. All over the world, most people are such slaves of tomorrow that they never really live today.

THE LIGHT OF LIFE

Why does God want us to stop worrying about tomorrow? Because whatever you worry about drives your life. Therefore, if you are worried about your needs, your needs begin to drive your life. Your needs become the devil's trap to distract you from fulfilling your God-given destiny. Making us worry about tomorrow is the devil's plan to distract us, so that we miss God's destiny for us. In other words, you become needs-driven, not destiny-driven. This causes you to miss your true destiny.

Jesus saw that the devil was using worry as a weapon to wreck God's plans for His people. That was why He said, "Do not worry about tomorrow." Those who don't worry about tomorrow are not easily trapped by the devil.

Let me illustrate this point with an example from my boyhood days. When I was growing up, I learned how to catch birds. I would go to a field, dig a hole, and pour water into it. Now, all along the birds had been happily fulfilling their purpose of flying in the sky but, when they saw the sparkling water, they became distracted by it. Suddenly it dawned upon them that they needed to drink this water, so down they flew.

This water had the effect of getting them to abort their true purpose (of flying in the sky) so that they could fulfil *my* purpose—to trap them. The birds stopped flying about in the sky and came down to drink the water, not knowing that they had fallen for my trick—and that was how I caught them.

This is exactly the same strategy the devil uses to distract us and make us miss our purpose on earth. He uses our needs to trap us and stop us from fulfilling our God-given purpose. This is nothing other than the devil's ploy to stop people from living for God's purposes. Worrying about tomorrow causes us to spend today making programmes for our tomorrows—which distracts us from seeing or fulfilling God's programme for us today. In other words, we are so programmed for tomorrow that we miss God's programme for today.

When Jesus said, "Do not worry about tomorrow," His intention was to prevent us from missing God's programme because of our own programmes. Worrying is the devil's best trap to destroy God's plans for us. When we are so distracted by continuously planning for tomorrow, we end up missing God's daily plan for us today.

The secret to discovering God's plan for your life

Until you abandon your own plans, you will never see God's plan for your life. This is a mystery that you need to understand. By clinging to your own plans, you are in effect destroying God's plan for your life. But if you abandon your own way, God will show you His way—it's as simple as that.

Most people have so many plans that they can't see God's plan for their lives, and these plans of theirs are thwarting God's plans for them. You cannot accomplish two different missions at the same time—you have to abandon one in order to accomplish the other. And this is what God wants us to do—to abandon our own plans so that He can give us His plan. Always remember that the only true plan for our lives is with Him. But we will only see God's plans on one condition—that we abandon our own plans.

As is written in the book of the words of Isaiah the prophet:

"A voice of one calling in the desert,
'Prepare the way for the Lord, make straight paths for him.'"

Luke 3:4

God's instructions to John the Baptist were to "go and tell the people that they should prepare the way for the Lord". In other words: "Tell the people to get themselves ready for God's way (plan) for their lives."

Now, how do I prepare myself for God's plan? By abandoning my own way (plan) in order to see God's way (plan). For this is the message that John was sent to deliver to the whole world: "Abandon your own plan and prepare yourself for God's plan."

For many years Christians have ignored John's message because they have not understood its meaning: that God is ready to reveal His plan to everyone, but only if we are ready to give up our own ways (plans). God does not reveal His plan to those who are still holding on to their own plans. Only to those who have abandoned their own plans for His sake will He reveal His plan.

Often, we are driven by the plans we have made for ourselves, not knowing that God has already prepared His plan for us, which is different from our own plans. Our plans are in conflict with God's plan, and this results in us missing God's plan for our lives.

You have the keys

Then Jesus said to his disciples, "If anyone would come after me, he must deny himself and take up his cross and follow me."

Matthew 16:24

What beautiful words from our Lord! If His disciples want to follow Him, they should first abandon their own plans—that is, forfeit their own ambitions, goals and purposes to pursue His purpose for their lives.

Taking up your cross means feeling the pain of giving up your own plans, ambitions and goals to follow God's plan. Giving up your own goals is never easy, but it opens the door to God's plan for you.

Denying your own plan is the key to unlocking God's plan for your life. On the other hand, holding on to your own plan is akin to locking up God's plan for your life and throwing away the key.

You have a choice: whether to open or shut the door to God's plan. Most people think God doesn't answer their prayers, but they don't know that God's answer to their prayers lies in their own hands. The key to your blessings is not with God but with you—God has already handed it to you. You can abandon God's destiny for you if you set your own plan above God's plan—that is not God's problem but yours.

All that God is waiting for us to do is to abandon our own way, so that He can open His way for us. You can pray ten times a day but, if you have rejected God's way, you will probably end up thinking God doesn't exist—because your prayers will not be answered. Not because God doesn't want to answer you, No! But because your own way has shut out God's answer for you. Let me repeat this again: *you have the keys to your destiny—not God—and you can choose to open the door to your own blessing or close it; it's up to you. You* have the keys.

"I will give you the keys of the kingdom of heaven; whatever you bind on earth will be bound in heaven, and whatever you loose on earth will be loosed in heaven."

Matthew 16:19

Most times, this verse has been misinterpreted. What does it actually mean? What Jesus meant was that, if you let go of (loose) your earthly plan, God's heavenly plan will also be released (loosed) to you. But if you hold on to (bind) your earthly plan, God's heavenly plan will in turn be withheld (bound) from you.

In other words, if you hold on to your earthly plan, God will not reveal His plan to you. But if you let go of your earthly plan, God will release and reveal to you His heavenly plan for your life. So you can now see that you really do hold the keys to God's plan for your life, whether to take hold of it or reject it.

To the extent that you hold on to your earthly plan, God also will hold on to His heavenly plan for your life; in other words, He will not reveal it to you. But when you release or let go of your own earthly plan, God also will release His own heavenly plan to you. So now you can see that indeed the keys are in your own hands and not God's.

"For whoever wants to save his life will lose it, but whoever loses his life for me will find it."
Matthew 16:25

To lose your life means to stop living for your own plans. This means you die to yourself by abandoning all your plans. You no longer live life for yourself. You release or let go of your plans for the sake of God's plans for your life. But if you hold on to your own plans, you will lose it all in the end—because God's plan for your life is eternal, whereas your plans are temporal. Your plans die when you die; but God's plan still lives on, even after your death.

So Elijah went from there and found Elisha son of Shaphat. He was ploughing with twelve yoke of oxen and he himself was driving the twelfth pair. Elijah went up to him and threw his cloak around him. Elisha then left his oxen and ran after Elijah. "Let me kiss my father and mother good-by," he said, "and then I will come with you."

"Go back," Elijah replied. "What have I done to you?"

So Elisha left him and went back. He took his yoke of oxen and slaughtered them. He burned the ploughing equipment to cook the meat and gave it to the people, and they ate. Then he set out to follow Elijah and became his attendant.

1 Kings 19:19-21

What do I want you to see from this passage of Scripture? First, Elisha was busy with his own plan of ploughing—he was busy with his own business. He had oxen and he himself was driving them. Secondly, when God called him, notice what he did: he went back, took his yoke of oxen and slaughtered them. Then he burned his ploughing equipment.

Why did he do all this? Because those things were his own plan and, when he found God's plan for his life, he abandoned his own plan in order to follow God's plan. This further illustrates my point: that the keys to God's plan for your life are in your own hands—you can choose to unlock the door, or lock it. It is entirely up to you.

The Lord had said to Abram, "Leave your country, your people and your father's household and go to the land I will show you.
"I will make you into a great nation and I will bless you; I will make your name great, and you will be a blessing."

Genesis 12:1-2

When God called Abraham, He made it clear to him that he should leave his country, his people and his father's house to follow God's plan for his life. What God was telling Abraham was that He had a plan for him, but that plan would only be revealed to him on one condition—he had to leave all he was doing in his home country.

God told Abraham that if he left his country, his people and his parents in order to follow His plan, God would surely bless him. But remember God's blessings could only be received on one condition—Abraham must leave his own plan for God's plan. The most difficult part for Abraham was to leave his country, people and parents for a place he did not even know.

God told Abraham He would show him the place to which He was taking him—a place as yet unknown to him. This again confirms that God will reveal His destiny for you—but only after you leave your own plans and pursue His plan. You will never know God's plan for your life until you die to yourself and abandon your own plans.

Although Abraham did not know where he was going, he trusted in the God who had called him. He left his own people, believing that God had a better plan for him—this is what we call faith. Abraham believed there was a better destiny ahead of him, although he could not see it.

God is looking for workers

Jesus posed these two questions to His disciples:

"What good will it be for a man if he gains the whole world, yet forfeits his soul? Or what can a man give in exchange for his soul?"

Matthew 16:26

What He was asking them was this: what good would it be for them to acquire everything in this world, if they missed God's plan for their lives? What good is that? God's purposes are actually the reason for our existence.

So why are you on this earth if you won't do what you were put here for? Most people complain about a lack of jobs, not knowing that God is looking for more workers in His kingdom.

Then he said to his disciples, "The harvest is plentiful but the workers are few. Ask the Lord of the harvest, therefore, to send out workers into his harvest field."
Matthew 9:37

There are plenty of jobs on earth, but they are hidden from our eyes. Lack of jobs is not the government's responsibility—as most people think—because we are not here for the government. We are here because God has already employed us for His work. If you weren't employed you wouldn't be on this earth. You are here because you are already employed by God.

Your responsibility is to find out what God has employed you to do. You cannot complain about lack of jobs to the government, because you weren't put on earth by the government—think about that.

Let's be honest: we cannot complain to the government about lack of jobs because they didn't put us here. They can't be held responsible for a lack of jobs—that's unfair to the government. We are here as workers for God's kingdom (although not everyone is employed by Him—only those who give their lives to live for His kingdom).

Father God is looking for workers, but sadly not everyone who comes to church can be considered a qualified worker—only those who commit themselves to live for His kingdom. You need to know, too, that it is not vitally important to be committed to your church (meaning, your church building) or pastor—that doesn't necessarily guarantee that you are serving in the kingdom of God. No! Not at all. But it *is* vitally important to commit your life to live for the kingdom of God.

Church commitment doesn't guarantee that you are indeed serving in the kingdom of God, but commitment to God's kingdom does. Perhaps church commitment might guarantee that you are serving in the church (that is, the church building), but not in the kingdom of God.

Your direction is in God—not yourself

Let us consider these words of the Psalmist David:

The LORD is my shepherd, I shall not be in want.
Psalms 23:1

This is something we can learn from David: he did not lead his own life, but God led him. God was his shepherd. A shepherd leads his flock in the direction he wants them to go. The sheep do not follow their own direction but the shepherd's. Because David was a shepherd himself, he understood the work that a shepherd did. And when David looked at his own life, he realized that he was like a sheep—because God was shepherding him and ensuring that he lived according to His plan.

David discovered this truth: he was not to go in his own direction, but in God's direction. He summed it up by saying, "The LORD is my shepherd." In other words, David was saying, "I'm not in control of my life; but God is in control of it." David's point was that we are all meant to follow the destiny God has prepared for us.

"I shall not be in want." What David meant was this: "Even though I might be in want now, when I reach the destiny God is shepherding me to, I shall not be in want." We might be in want now, but our destiny has been prepared with everything we want, and when we reach our destiny we shall not be in want. Let me tell you something: there is nothing wrong with being in want now because, when you reach the green pastures to which God is shepherding you, you shall never be in want. Because everything has been prepared for you there!

When God was shepherding the Israelites to the Promised Land, they were in want of a lot of things on the way there. Most of them could not see what the Promised Land had in store for them. They did not know that, in the land to which God was shepherding them, they would never be in want. It is the same with many of God's children—they get discouraged on the road before they reach their Promised Land. Therefore, they never reach their Promised Land.

The Light of Life

Even though I walk through the valley
　of the shadow of death,
I will fear no evil, for you are with me;
　your rod and your staff, they comfort me.

Psalms 23:4

Here David was saying that, even though sometimes the road was rough, he was not afraid because he knew it wasn't his destiny; it was just the road that led him to his destiny. In other words, the road which leads you to your destiny is not always an easy or pleasant one. It might go up mountains or down through valleys, but one thing you should understand—the road passes through those places, but those places aren't the destination itself.

So do not confuse the road with the destination, as the Israelites did. The road might be bad, but your destiny is much better. When the Israelites were on the road to the Promised Land, they complained many times to God, saying they wanted to go back to Egypt. This was because they couldn't see the treasure that was their destiny.

God has treasures for us too, in the Promised Land to which He is leading us. He has better plans for you than you can ever have for yourself. All you need is to give your life to Him, and He will show you better and greater things.

CHAPTER 11

Destiny Is Not Instant but God's Planned Process

Some time later the brook dried up because there had been no rain in the land. Then the word of the LORD came to him: "Go at once to Zarephath of Sidon and stay there. I have commanded a widow in that place to supply you with food." So he went to Zarephath. When he came to the town gate, a widow was there gathering sticks. He called to her and asked, "Would you bring me a little water in a jar so I may have a drink?" As she was going to get it, he called, "And bring me, please, a piece of bread.

"As surely as the LORD your God lives," she replied, "I don't have any bread—only a handful of flour in a jar and a little oil in a jug. I am gathering a few sticks to take home and make a meal for myself and my son, that we may eat it—and die."

Elijah said to her, "Don't be afraid. Go home and do as you have said. But first make a small cake of bread for me, and then make something for yourself and your son. For this is what the LORD, the God of Israel, says: 'The jar of flour will not be used up and the jug of oil will not run dry until the day the LORD gives rain on the land.'"

She went away and did as Elijah had told her. So there was food every day for Elijah and for the woman and her family. For the jar of flour was not used up and the jug of oil did not run dry, in keeping with the word of the LORD spoken by Elijah.

1 Kings 17:7-16

Now notice something about this widow: she went to bed the previous night without sticks to make a fire, and she wasn't worried about it until she woke up in the morning. Then she realized she didn't have sticks to bake a cake. The need of that day (for sticks) drove her to the field and, as she was in the field gathering the sticks, she met Elijah.

Imagine what would have happened if she had collected the sticks before she went to bed the previous night—she wouldn't have woken up with the need to go to the field. She would have missed meeting Elijah, and thereby missed out on God's provision for her needs. Think about that. So what she needed for that day led her to God's blessings for her.

In other words, her tomorrows weren't programmed. Therefore, she saw God's programme for her life for that day, which led her to God's blessings for her. She went to bed without sticks to bake bread for tomorrow, but she didn't worry about it—she would face tomorrow's needs when tomorrow came, and not today. I hope you can now see what Jesus meant when He said, "Do not worry about tomorrow, for tomorrow will worry about itself. Each day has enough trouble of its own." *(Matthew 6:34)*

Each day has enough problems of its own—problems that will lead you to God's blessings for you. The woman's problem of not having firewood led to her being blessed by God through Elijah. If she hadn't encountered that problem, she wouldn't have been blessed; she wouldn't have gone to the field to gather sticks. So do not worry about tomorrow, but let each day come with its own needs, and those needs will lead you to God's blessings for you.

Unfortunately, most people want to face tomorrow's needs today. Their minds are always so programmed for tomorrow that they do not see God's programme for today. In fact, God's children often miss today's blessings because their minds are always programmed for tomorrow.

One day, after Moses had grown up, he went out to where his own people were and watched them at their hard labour. He saw an Egyptian beating a Hebrew, one of his own people. Glancing this way and that and seeing no one, he killed the Egyptian and hid him in the sand. The next day he went out and saw the two Hebrews fighting. He asked the one in the wrong, "Why are you hitting your fellow Hebrew?"

The man said, "Who made you ruler and judge over us? Are you thinking of killing me as you killed the Egyptian?"

Then Moses was afraid and thought, "What I did must have become known."

When Pharaoh heard of this, he tried to kill Moses, but Moses fled from Pharaoh and went to live in Midian, where he sat down by a well. Now a priest of Midian had seven daughters, and they came to draw water and fill the troughs to water their father's flock. Some shepherds came along and drove them away, but Moses got up and came to their rescue and watered their flock. When the girls return to Reuel their father, he asked them, "Why have you returned so early today?"

They answered, "An Egyptian rescued us from the shepherds. He even drew water for us and watered the flock."

"And where is he?" he asked his daughters. "Why did you leave him?" Invite him to have something to eat."

Moses agreed to stay with the man, who gave his daughter Zipporah to Moses in marriage.

Exodus 2:11-21

I want us to see where Moses' destiny started: it began the day he killed the Egyptian. Now, this killing didn't happen by accident but it was God working out His plan for Moses. After the killing, Pharaoh heard about it and wanted to kill Moses for what he did.

Consider this: Moses didn't wake up with a plan to kill the Egyptian. It just happened that he saw the Egyptian beating one of his own people. Now the trouble that Moses caused on that day—killing the Egyptian—led to Pharaoh wanting to kill him. But, as Moses was running away from Pharaoh, he was running towards his destiny. As he was running to his destiny, he found his wife on the way to his destiny.

You see, the trouble that caused Moses to run away also caused him to find his wife on the way to his destiny. If that trouble hadn't happened, Moses wouldn't have met his wife. Moses didn't search for his wife, but his wife was placed on the way to his destiny—can you see that? Can you see the wisdom of God in the way He orchestrated these events? So you don't have to search for the things you want, but only for your destiny—because the things you want are found on the way to your destiny.

Our own programmes will cause us to miss God's programme for us. Moses was being led by God's programme because he didn't have a personal programme for that day; the trouble of that day became God's programme for him. In other words, Moses' need of the day (for a new home), led him to find a wife; as Moses was searching for a new home after he left Egypt, he met his wife Zipporah. So do not seek after things, but seek God's plan, which will lead you to the things you want.

Listen to what Jesus said:

"But seek first his kingdom and his righteousness, and all these things will be given to you as well."

Matthew 6:33

Moses' experience testifies to the truth of Jesus' words—as he was moving according to God's direction, he met his wife. Moses wasn't searching for his wife. He was on the way to his destiny, and the road to his destiny led him to where his wife was. So do not search for things but for your destiny—because you will find the things you need on the way to your destiny.

The Light of Life

What I want to show you is that our daily needs drive us to God's destiny for us. Everything that happened in Egypt was for the purpose of moving Moses from Egypt to Midian. Consider something else: as Moses was shepherding his father-in-law's flock, the flock caused him to go to the mountain of God, where he met the Lord. So God used the flock to take Moses to the place where He wanted to meet him. If it wasn't for the flock, Moses wouldn't have gone up the mountain—the flock was the reason Moses went to the mountain of God.

In the end, everything that happened to Moses led him into finding God's plan for his life. The wisdom of God is far beyond our understanding. His plans for us are far beyond our own plans. God has a better plan for each of us than we have for ourselves; He wants to bless us abundantly, far beyond what we can imagine. But he does it His way, not your way—actually your way hinders God's way for your life.

For our light and momentary troubles are achieving for us an eternal glory that far outweighs them all. So we fix our eyes not on what is seen, but on what is unseen. For what is seen is temporary, but what is unseen is eternal.
2 Corinthians 4:17-18

Remember this: as a child of God, all the troubles that you face in your life—whether at home, at work, in the street, or anywhere else—are not there to destroy you, but to make you who you should be. They have been put there because, if they don't happen to you, you won't be able to fulfil your destiny. So don't fight against your tests and trials—let them fulfil the purpose they have been sent to accomplish. Remember that they are not there to destroy you but to mould you into the person you should be.

> *This is the word that came to Jeremiah from the* LORD: *"Go down to the potter's house, and there I will give you my message."*
>
> *So I went down to the potter's house, and I saw him working at the wheel. But the pot he was shaping from the clay was marred in his hands; so the potter formed it into another pot, shaping it as seemed best to him.*
>
> *Then the word of the* LORD *came to me: "O house of Israel, can I not do with you as this potter does?" declares the* LORD. *"Like clay in the hand of the potter, so are you in my hand, O house of Israel."*
>
> Jeremiah 18:1-6

When God sent Jeremiah to the potter's house, He said that He wanted to give him a message. What was the message God wanted to give him? It was this: the clay doesn't know the design the potter wants; only the potter does.

So it is with us. We don't know the purpose for which God has put us here on earth; only God knows. So whatever happens in our lives is working to shape us for the purposes God has for us.

Sometimes it seems like the potter is destroying the clay. But the truth is, his plan is not to destroy it but to mould it into what he purposed it to be. Sometimes the potter even puts the clay in the fire, not to destroy it, but to strengthen and transform it into the beautiful vessel he had designed it to be.

So it is with us: we are like clay in God's hands, and He is our Potter. Whatever happens in our lives, we need to remember that the Potter knows what He is doing—not the clay. The clay should simply trust the Potter. The design doesn't lie in the clay itself, but with the Potter. So it is with God's purposes for us; it is not known to us but only to God.

You are directed to your destiny through other people: good and bad, Christians and non-Christians

Now Moses was tending the flock of Jethro his father-in-law, the priest of Midian, and he led the flock to the far side of the desert and came to Horeb, the mountain of God. There the angel of the LORD appeared to him in flames of fire from within a bush.

Moses saw that though the bush was on fire it did not burn up. So Moses thought, "I will go over and see this strange sight—why the bush does not burn up.

When the LORD saw that he had gone over to look, God called to him from within the bush, "Moses! Moses!"

And Moses said, "Here I am."

Exodus 3:1-4

Let us take another look at Moses' road to his destiny. Consider this: Moses was given the task of looking after his father-in-law's flock. But who was really the one who gave him the task? Jethro—or God?

God wanted Moses to meet Him on the mountain; and, because of this, He moved Jethro to give Moses the job of looking after his flock. So one day, while doing his job, Moses took his father-in-law's flock to graze on Horeb, the mountain of God. And while he was on this mountain, he met the Lord—can you see how his shepherding work led him to meet God?

Now, learn this from Moses' life: no matter what kind of work people ask you to do, do it with all your might—because you never know what God has planned for you through that job! Don't complain or grumble, but do your work with a joyful heart. If you refuse to do it, you might be refusing God's plan for your life; it might be that God is taking you to your destiny through that work.

Imagine what would have happened if Moses had refused to do the work of shepherding which his father-in-law requested him to do. He would have missed his destiny—think about that. Moses was humble enough to do what Jethro asked him to do— and, in so doing, he was led to his destiny. Most people are too proud to acquiesce to other people's requests, and so they miss what could have been God's destiny for their lives. Pride has caused many people to miss their own destiny.

The Light of Life

During the time Mordecai was sitting at the king's gate, Bigthana and Teresh, two of the king's officers who guarded the doorway, became angry and conspired to assassinate King Xerxes. But Mordecai found out about the plot and told Queen Esther, who in turn reported it to the king, giving credit to Mordecai. And when the report was investigated and found to be true, the two officials were hanged on a gallows. All this was recorded in the book of the annals in the presence of the king.

Esther 2:21-23

In the scripture passage above, we learn that Mordecai was given the job of a guard at the king's gate. This does not seem be work that most people would like to do, but Mordecai took it on.

Now consider the plan of God behind Mordecai's job: God put Mordecai in that position so that he could find out about the plot to assassinate the king. God knew what was going to happen, and He placed Mordecai there for this one purpose: so that he would be in the right place when the two officers guarding the doorway were planning to kill the king. So Mordecai overheard the whole plot and reported it to Queen Esther.

But when Mordecai was given the job, he had no idea what God was planning by placing him there! So this is the reason I say to you, whatever people ask you to do, just do it with all your heart—because you never know what could be God's plan behind it all.

You might be headed for better things through that request. Consider what Mordecai received in the end, as a result of what he did:

Mordecai the Jew was second in rank to King Xerxes, preeminent among the Jews, and held in high esteem by his many fellow Jews, because he worked for the good of his people and spoke up for the welfare of all the Jews.

Esther 10:3

Actually, most people miss God's plan for their lives because they are too proud to do the work given to them; they will only do the work that suits them. Don't let pride cause you to miss God's destiny for your life!

Let us take a look now into the life of David when he was still a shepherd boy:

Now Jesse said to his son David, "Take this ephah of roasted grain and these ten loaves of bread for your brothers and hurry to their camp. Take along these ten cheeses to the commander of their unit. See how your brothers are and bring back some assurance from them. They are with Saul and all the men of Israel in the Valley of Elah, fighting against the Philistines."

Early in the morning David left the flock with a shepherd, loaded up and set out, as Jesse had directed. He reached the camp as the army was going out to its battle positions, shouting the war cry. Israel and the Philistines were drawing up their lines facing each other. David left his things with the keeper of supplies, ran to the battle lines and greeted his brothers. As he was talking with them, Goliath, the Philistine champion from

Gath, stepped out from his lines and shouted his usual defiance, and David heard it. When the Israelites saw the man, they all ran from him in great fear.

Now the Israelites had been saying, "Do you see how this man keeps coming out? He comes out to defy Israel. The king will give great wealth to the man who kills him. He will also give him his daughter in marriage and will exempt his father's family from taxes in Israel."

David asked the men standing near him, "What will be done for the man who kills this Philistine and removes this disgrace from Israel? Who is this uncircumcised Philistine that he should defy the armies of the living God?"

They repeated to him what they had been saying and told him, "This is what will be done for the man who kills him."

1 Samuel 17:17-27

Now, it wasn't by accident that David went to war and killed Goliath. Consider the timing of God's plan for David:

- ❖ David arrived at the camp as the Israelites and Philistines were going to their battle lines;

- ❖ He arrived at a time when Goliath was shouting out his usual defiance.

God planned that day long before anyone else knew about it. God used David's father Jesse to send him to the warfront as a boy taking food to his brothers. David had no idea that he was going to his destiny; he thought it was all about delivering food to his brothers and returning home. But God's plan was different—it was far bigger than what David or his father had in mind.

Many would have refused to go on such a simple mission, but David was willing to be a delivery boy. What about you? Do you think you would have gone—just to deliver food? Be honest with yourself.

Imagine what would have happened if David had refused his father's request. He would not have gone to the warfront and heard about Goliath. He would not have fought him. Eventually David became king as a result of his victory over Goliath.

It is unlikely that David could have achieved as much in his life as he did, if he had not defeated Goliath. But because he was willing to serve his brothers humbly as a delivery boy, he fulfilled God's plan for his life—and what a great plan it was!

Again I repeat: don't live your life for things, but live it for your destiny. Things are found when you find your destiny—David's life is a testimony to this truth. David wasn't looking for things, but he found the things he needed, the day he found his destiny.

CHAPTER 12

God's Grace

The subject of God's grace has been misinterpreted most of the time. What does the word "grace" mean? It can be defined this way: "extra time allowed to do something after the date when it is due to be done; for example, to renew a license or pay a bill". Grace is an extended period of time granted as a special favor to someone to renew or pay what is due after its due (expiry) date.

In other words, the grace given to us is an extended time of God's favor to renew what was due. What is it that was due? It was man's life. When man disobeyed God's command and ate from the forbidden tree, he destroyed his own life. He could no longer do what he was created to do, because he had lost his true origin. He could no longer serve God's purposes; therefore his life was at its due (expiry) date.

But God by His grace chose to give man a new birth. God was under no obligation to rebirth us, but it was His own choice to resurrect that which was due (dead)—man's life. This is called grace because God was not building a new thing, but He was renewing what was due (man's life).

God's Grace

It was God's grace that sent Christ to earth to pay the price for man's redemption (by dying on the cross) and to renew man's life. Grace is God's favor upon us, so that we can regain the life that was lost when Adam fell—this is the true meaning of grace. God gave us another opportunity to regain the identity we had before the fall.

To illustrate: suppose you bought a car from a car dealer, and you were paying for it in instalments. And suppose you ran into financial difficulties, to the point where you could not afford to pay the instalments anymore. As a result, the car dealer decided to repossess the car, because you failed to pay the instalment on the date it was due.

Now suppose, after a little while, the car dealer informed you that you could still regain the car if you were to pay a certain amount to cover the instalment that was due. This means that the dealer allowed you extra time—a grace period—to pay up. This is the grace given to you by the car dealer. It is grace because the car dealer was not obligated to give you that extra opportunity to regain the car.

This is the same kind of grace that God has given to mankind. In Christ, God has given us an extra opportunity to regain the life that we lost because of Adam's fall.

The Light of Life

"Now I commit you to God and to the word of his grace, which can build you up and give you an inheritance…"
Acts 20:32

I would like you to understand fully the import of Paul's words in *Acts 20:32* above. Let me share this illustration with you: suppose you had always been in good health, but suddenly you fell sick and decided to go to the doctor. What made you go to the doctor? Your sickness—and your desire to get well again.

When you got to the doctor, he examined you and prescribed treatment for you. Why? So that, by following the doctor's prescription, you could rebuild your health and regain the healthy body you had lost. Following the doctor's prescription would guarantee you a restoration of your health.

So it is the same with following God's prescription (His Word); it guarantees us a restoration of the kind of life lost by Adam in the fall. After accepting Christ as our Lord and Savior, we have to abide by God's Word. By practicing God's Word in our lives, we rebuild the life that was lost through Adam's fall.

So when Paul said, "I commit you to God and to the word of his grace, which can build you up and give you an inheritance," he was actually saying, "I commit you to God and to the word of His grace, which is able to rebuild in you the life you lost through the fall."

Notice too that Paul used the word *inheritance*. What inheritance was he talking about? He was referring to the administration of the earth that was lost through Adam's fall. This was the same administration that God used to create the universe, and it was also given to mankind by God the Father, so that we could be administrators of the earth. Paul called it an "inheritance" because it belonged to God the Father, who gave it to His children.

Paul meant that, by allowing God's Word to guide you in your daily life, it will rebuild you to the point where you have the power of God and are able to take hold of the inheritance that had been lost by Adam's fall. There is a building process you need to undergo. Just as the doctor gives you his prescription to rebuild your health, so God gives you His Word to rebuild your life—so that, by practicing the Word of His grace, you will regain the life lost by Adam in the fall.

It is not enough just to have His grace; you need to do what the Word prescribed—just as it is not enough simply to go to the doctor, without doing what the doctor prescribed. The reason most Christians do not regain their inheritance is that they do not act on the Word of God's grace. It is like going to the doctor but neglecting to act on his prescription. You will never find your healing—because the healing actually lies in the prescription.

The Prayer of Repentance

All the good things I talked about in this book are only for God's children—that is, all who have been born again into the Kingdom of God by acknowledging Jesus as their Lord and Savior. If you are not yet a child of God and would like to be, please pray the following prayer:

Heavenly Father, I have come to the understanding that you are truly the Lord of my life. You have opened my eyes to see the truth; I now believe that Jesus Christ is your Son and that you have sent Him to save sinners, of whom I am one. I acknowledge that I am a sinner and I need your salvation. Jesus Christ, come into my heart; make me one with you, save me from my life of sin. Amen.

Questions? Comments?

Write to Reginald Nedzamba

Email: reginald.nedzamba@yahoo.com

Facebook: Reginald Nedzamba

www.ingramcontent.com/pod-product-compliance
Lightning Source LLC
Chambersburg PA
CBHW061656040426
42446CB00010B/1769